MERCHANTS OF DEATH
GLOBAL OLIGARCHS AND THEIR WAR ON HUMANITY

PROFESSOR JOHN GIDEON HARTNETT

PROFESSOR AUGUSTO ZIMMERMANN

FOREWORD BY
GABRIËL A. MOENS AM

FOREWORD BY
STEVE CIOCCOLANTI

U S A
P R E S S

"Don't call everything a conspiracy, like they do, and don't live in dread of what frightens them. Make the Lord of Heaven's Armies holy in your life. He is the one you should fear. He is the one who should make you tremble."

ISAIAH 8:12-13 (NLT)

"And you shall know the truth, and the truth shall make you free."

JOHN 8:32

CONTENTS

ABOUT THE AUTHORS

Professor John Gideon Hartnett is an Australian physicist, cosmologist and Christian author with a biblical, creationist worldview. He earned a Ph.D. in Physics (with distinction) from The University of Western Australia. He has published more than 200 research papers in leading scientific journals, book chapters and conference proceedings. He is the recipient of ARC Discovery Outstanding Researcher Award (DORA) fellowship at the University of Adelaide. He was a founding director of an Australian start-up, now commercializing his world leading research on ultra-stable cryogenic 'sapphire clocks'. These clocks have formed part of Australia's over-the-horizon-radar defense system known as Jindalee Operational Radar Network (JORN). In 2010 he received the W.G. Cady Award which recognizes outstanding contributions in the fields of piezoelectric or other classical frequency control, selection and measurement and resonant sensor devices. The citation reads: "for the construction of ultra-stable cryogenic sapphire dielectric resonator oscillators and promotion of their applications in the fields of frequency metrology and radio-astronomy."

John writes topical articles on biblical creation science, particularly on astronomy and cosmology, and other biblically relevant subjects. He has contributed numerous articles to the *Answers Research Journal* (Answers in Genesis), the *Journal of*

Creation, Creation Magazine (Creation Ministries International) and Creation.com.

He has written two books, *Dismantling the Big Bang,* published by Master Books (USA) and *Starlight Time and the New Physics,* published by Creation Book Publishers (USA). He has also produced many DVDs on biblical creation lectures he has given. He has contributed to the *Epoch Times, The Spectator Australia, Caldron Pool* and Mises.org. John has lectured around the world in churches and conferences (secular topics and biblical apologetics).

He blogs at https://johnhartnett.org and https://BibleScienceForum.com.

See:

https://creation.com/dr-john-hartnett
https://creation.com/dr-john-hartnett-cv
http://creationwiki.org/John_Hartnett
https://adelaide.academia.edu/JohnHartnett
https://www.conservapedia.com/John_Hartnett
https://en.wikipedia.org/wiki/John_Hartnett_(physicist)

Professor Augusto Zimmermann, PhD (Monash) is Law Professor and Head of Law at Sheridan Institute of Higher Education, in Perth, Western Australia. He is the former Director of Postgraduate Research (2011-2012 and 2015-2017) and the former Associate Dean, Research (2010-2012) at Murdoch Law School. During his time at Murdoch, Dr Zimmermann was awarded the University's Vice Chancellor's Award for Excellence in Research in 2012.

He is also a former Commissioner with the Law Reform Commission of Western Australia (2012-2017), President of the Western Australian Legal Theory Association (WALTA), a former Vice-President of the Australasian Society of Legal Philosophy (ASLP), an Elected Fellow at the International Academy for the Study of the Jurisprudence of the Family (IASJF), and Editor-in-Chief of The Western Australian Jurist law journal.

A prolific writer and the author of numerous articles and academic books, Professor Zimmermann was awarded two School Dean's Research Awards in 2010 and 2011. He served on numerous academic bodies at Murdoch, including: the Research Degree and Scholarships Committee; the Vice Chancellor's Awards and Citations Committee; the Academic Council's Freedom of Speech in Policies and Procedures Advisory Group; and the Academic Staff Promotions Advisory Committee.

In January 2015, he was invited by the Tasmanian Chief Justice to address the 'Opening of the Legal Year' in that State. Professor Zimmermann is generally recognized as a fierce advocate for freedom of speech and the Rule of Law, contributing with numerous articles on the subject, including for *The Legal Doctrines of the Rule of Law and the Legal State* (Rechtshaid) (Springer, 2014), a book edited by the President of the American Bar Association (ABA) that explores the development of both the civil law and the common law conceptions of the Rule of Law.

He is the author/co-author/editor/co-editor of numerous academic articles and books, including

- *The Spirit behind the Voice: The Religious Dimension of the "Voice" Proposal,* Connor Court Publishing, 2023;
- *Foundations of the Australian Legal System: History, Theory and Practice,* LexisNexis, 2023;
- *Wokeshevism: Critical Theories and the Tyrant Left,* Connor Court Publishing 2023;
- *Fundamental Rights in the Age of Covid-19,* Connor Court Publishing, 2021;
- *No Offence Intended: Why 18C is Wrong,* Connor Court Publishing, 2016;
- *Christian Foundations of the Common Law (3 Volumes),* Connor Court Publishing, 2018;
- *Global Perspectives on Subsidiarity,* Springer, 2014; and
- *Western Legal Theory: History, Concepts and Perspectives,* LexisNexis, 2013.

Professor Zimmermann contributes on various legal, cultural and political matters for RT, The Spectator, Quadrant, The Epoch Times and several other newspapers. He has been included, together with only twelve other Australian academics and policy experts, in 'Policy Experts' – the Heritage Foundation's directory for locating knowledgeable authorities and leading policy institutes actively involved in a broad range of public policy issues, both in the United States and worldwide.

For the latest updates on his writings go to: https://walta.net.au

PUBLISHER'S NOTE
STEVE CIOCCOLANTI, B.A., M.ED.

Professors John Hartnett and **Augusto Zimmermann**'s book is being released to the public at a tipping point when the evidence against the Elites' corruption and crimes against humanity is becoming so overwhelming, high-ranking ministers and their advisors are scrambling to conduct damage control and hide the truth at any cost, even discrediting and arresting whistleblowers.

At the end of 2023, New Zealander Barry Young discovered inconsistent and hidden information in his government's Covid-19 vaccination data. For no personal gain, but in the interest of public health and safety, Young released the forbidden data to the public, enraging the oligarchs of the socialist island nation. I am convinced that the candor of the two professors, combined with their academic credibility and quality research, could make them public enemy #1 to some in the ruling class of Australia.

I salute the authors for taking a heroic stand to document the incomplete path to tyranny undertaken during the COVID pandemic, and to warn us that the oligarchs—the Merchants of

Death—have not given up on their plans. In fact, the Bible informs us that this was only their "dry run." They're going to make another attempt at health totalitarianism, just as the Nazis tried to do in Germany. Ultimately the leader who succeeds in foisting this technocratic control over the world will be worse than Adolf Hitler. He will be the Anti-Christ about whom ancient prophecies have long warned.

Professors John Hartnett and Augusto Zimmermann have drawn from their depth of academic experience to produce a well-researched counter-offensive to Klaus Schwab's Great Reset. The conspiracies of the Elites are no longer secret. In his book, "Covid-19: The Great Reset," Schwab openly applauded pandemics, calling the Black Death that killed upwards of 200 million people "the unrecognized beginning of modern man." Schwab longed for another pandemic to usher in "long-lasting and dramatic consequences for our world today" and wrote, "we should take advantage of this unprecedented opportunity to reimagine our world."[1] Many in the World Economic Forum (WEF) agree with him. For such reasons, the professors have identified Schwab as one of the "Merchants of Death."

As the apparatus of the One World police state become increasingly enhanced by Big Tech, Big Data, global surveillance, artificial intelligence and the globally-controlled, monolithic media/ social media, the warnings in this book will move in scale from cautioning the innocents against a transient hiccup in normality to alarming the Bride of Christ against being enslaved by the Anti-Christ and the Mark of the Beast (aka 'the New Normal'). Your eternal soul, not merely your health, will be at stake. In this book is the forbidden information you're not supposed to know. Consume it, and it will lead you away from the corrupt leaders who plan to enslave you and to safety of the only Savior Jesus Christ who wants to set you free.

FOREWORD
GABRIËL A. MOENS AM

John Gideon Hartnett and Augusto Zimmermann, both noted and accomplished columnists and academics, have collaborated to describe the totalitarian agenda of the oligarchs. They imaginatively, but not inaccurately, describe the 'oligarchs' as the 'Merchants of Death'. The subtitle of their book, *Global Oligarchs and their War on Humanity*, reveals the book's focus: the various tools these merchants use to wage war on humanity for the purpose of establishing a New World Order.

Nowadays, the word 'oligarch' has a pejorative meaning. Journalists usually describe 'oligarchs' as people whose prurient tastes and corporate activities nourish the often decadent lifestyle of President Vladimir Putin's confidants. In this sense, the word 'oligarchs' describes Russian billionaires who, after the collapse of the Soviet Union in 1991, sought to control the decaying communist institutions, including banking, oil, agriculture, and mining, thus becoming fabulously wealthy.

These Russian 'oligarchs' were able to maintain their enviable lifestyle as long as they remained loyal to Putin.

However, when Putin started his ill-conceived 'special military operation' in Ukraine, their fortunes started to decline. Their Western assets, such as luxurious yachts and villas, were often seized, and their bank accounts frozen, as part of the sanctions the West imposed on Russia for its invasion of Ukraine. The confiscations of the property of the 'oligarchs' implied that wealthy Russians who were close to the Kremlin were corrupt and tainted by the invasion of Ukraine. In this context, Al Tompkins estimates that "Russian oligarchs laundered $2.3 billion in real estate, jewelry, art and yachts in the last five years" and that they often "use shell companies and complex corporate structures to hide the assets." [1]

The confiscation of the Western assets of the 'oligarchs' is based on the discredited theory that a person must be guilty by association, and in this case, by association with the Kremlin. It is ironic that, since the Ukraine war, Russian oligarchs suffer from potentially illicit confiscations of assets which themselves were obtained by dubious practices after the fall of communism in Russia. In the United States, confiscation of illegally obtained wealth is certainly legal under the *Civil Asset Forfeiture Reform Act* of 2000, which has its roots in the 18th century when America would seize cargo from foreign ships that failed to pay a customs duty or import tax. Nowadays, seizure of assets is a tool used in the war against drug smugglers; it is also a formidable weapon used against terrorists.

In this captivating book, the word 'oligarchs' refers to persons who wield their great political or corporate power to impose their preferred opinions on others, thereby demeaning personal freedom and integrity, which are undeniably important achievements of Western civilisation. Hence, the word is not limited to describing the rich and wealthy who profited from the collapse of the Soviet Union, but instead encompasses the 'illiberal elites' who use their power, wealth, and influence to oppress Western civilisation in the pursuit of an utopian world government.

The book is a stark reminder that "the world is filled with superficiality, prejudice, bias, distortions, lies, deception, manipulation, short sightedness, close-mindedness, righteousness, hypocrisy … in every culture in every country throughout the world" leading to "fear, anxiety, sadness, hopelessness, pain, suffering, injustices of every imaginable kind." [2]

Although the present woke society–nourished by relentless social-engineering legislation adopted by compliant parliaments–is omnipresent, Western oligarchs and oligarchical behavior have always existed. Indeed, even in the middle of the 19th century, the celebrated philosopher and politician, John Stuart Mill, in his essay *On Liberty* wrote that governments tend to diminish the rights of people, and that the only bulwark against tyranny and oppression is moral conviction and line drawing by those concerned with the maintenance of freedom. He prophetically stated:

"[T]here is also in the world at large an increasing inclination to stretch unduly the powers of society over the individual, both by the force of opinion and even by that of legislation; and as the tendency of all the changes taking place in the world is to strengthen society, and diminish the power of the individual, this encroachment is not one of the evils which tend spontaneously to disappear, but, on the contrary, to grow more and more formidable. The disposition of mankind, whether as rulers or as fellow-citizens, to impose their own opinions and inclinations as a rule of conduct on others, is so energetically supported by some of the best and by some of the worst feelings incident to human nature, that it is hardly ever kept under restraint … and as the power is not declining, but growing, unless a strong barrier of moral conviction

can be raised against the mischief, we must expect, in the present circumstances of the world, to see it increase". [3]

Mill's analysis aptly and relevantly describes the horrendous violations of people's rights during the COVID-19 pandemic, revealing an invidious trend to authoritarianism in Australia. He derides sheep-like conformity which enables rulers, policymakers and trendsetters to impose their controlling views and arbitrary rules on people: "The only freedom which deserves the name, is that of pursuing our own good in our own way, so long as we do not attempt to deprive others of theirs, or impede their efforts to obtain it." [4]

Mill signals that it is imprudent to allow 'oligarchs' to decide what is harmful, especially if they are allocated a wide, uncontrolled power capable of silencing any dissent in society.

Hartnett's and Zimmermann's book constitutes a treasure trove of ideas, and it reminds people that ideas are, at least potentially, powerful tools to repel the global madness–the Great Reset–promoted by the World Economic Forum and infecting mankind. President Ronald Reagan was right when, in his inaugural address on 20 January 1981, he stated that "Government is not the solution to our problem, government is the problem." Reagan's aphorism is a powerful reminder that tyranny is very close to freedom because freedom can easily be obliterated in a single generation.

The book is a splendid example of how courageous academics can inform people about the real or perceived dangers of oligarchical behavior that threatens freedom. Surely, the ruling illiberal elites will describe the interesting insights of the authors of the book as 'disinformation' – the kind of information that illiberal governments would seek to ban by their relentless imposition of obnoxious 'misinformation' and 'disinformation' legislation on people. However, such characterisations of their book do not diminish the potent force of the arguments and views presented by the authors. I strongly recommend this book to all who are concerned about the maintenance of Western civilization. The book contains useful information, compelling arguments, and rich ideas which will open readers' eyes to the devastation wrought upon our civilization by those who pursue their illiberal, 'oligarchical', frightening agenda that is already devouring our world.

Emeritus Professor Gabriël A. Moens AM
JD (Leuven), LLM (Northwestern), PhD (Sydney),
GCEd (Queensland), MBA (Murdoch), MAppL (COL),
FCIArb, CIArb, FAIM, FCL, FAAL
Ghent (Belgium), 8 August 2023

PREFACE

June 1, 2023, The Western Australian front page headlines openly stating the existence of The New World Order, which has been denied for many decades.

For years, the term *New World Order* has been used to represent a hypothesis arguing that the world will one day be ruled by a totalitarian order. The *New World Order,* spoken about at various times in the past, was always treated by the mainstream media as a *conspiracy theory.* Anyone who spoke of the existence of such a conspiracy was treated as a nut job. Yet over the years, US presidents, corporate leaders and government elites in many Western countries have used these three words publicly.

In September 2021, Dr Kerry Chant, the chief health adviser in New South Wales (NSW), announced: "We will be looking at what contact tracing looks like in the new world order".[1]

Was this a slip of the tongue from the state's chief health officer? Perhaps not. After all, the notorious former NSW Liberal Health Minister, Brad Hazzard, had uttered the same phrase a few months before. "We've got to accept this is the new world order", he said on July 30, 2021.[2]

Was that a signal to their cronies? We don't know, but you shouldn't have any doubts any longer because we hear and see the expression *New World Order* everywhere now. Of course, if Dr Chant and Mr Hazzard are part of a project to impose global, totalitarian rule, it appears sloppy of them to mention its existence on live TV, directed at the very people they hope to subjugate.

However, the way the global oligarchs often portray their *New World Order* is that it would bring in a new order in the world which would be beneficial to all. Global oligarchs use this term 'new world order' to communicate a turning point in history. But as we have learned from the 3 years of tyranny under the sorcery of the COVID-19 "pandemic", what the oligarchs tell you they are doing is the exact opposite of what they are actually doing. We cannot be fooled any longer.

In this book we explain who the oligarchs are and their

agenda. We elaborate on the World Economic Forum's neo-fascist agenda and its plans for world domination with one global government after a *Great Reset* of the world's economic, social and governance systems (chapter 1). The oligarchs engineered a "pandemic" to kick off their *Great Reset* by using a fake healthcare scare to get mass compliance through fear. Like any good communist revolution, they had to destroy the old world order to introduce their totalitarian *New World Order*. Parallels are drawn with former communist revolutions. And like any good communist takeover, the oligarchs need to reduce the world population while surveilling and controlling the rest of us (chapter 2).

The opening salvo in their depopulation program was genetically-engineered bioweapons, or more precisely, a virus engineered to be more infectious to humans, followed by a toxic shot called a vaccine. However, that program, though causing millions of injuries and deaths worldwide, would prove not as effective as hoped. What followed, and sometimes simultaneously, were concomitant methods like engineered famine (chapter 3), social, economic and kinetic wars (chapter 4) and "plagues" of sterilization, mutilation of children, abortion, euthanasia and destruction of human fertility, all in the name of saving the planet from a mythical problem called "climate change" (chapters 5 and 6).

Destroying all methods of human survival on this planet through destruction of mental and physical health, productive labor and income (engineered financial collapse), food production (war on carbon dioxide), supply chains, weather warfare, and kinetic wars is very high on their agenda. Of course, this is all done in the name of saving the planet from the most serious plague: humanity (chapter 7). We are the carbon they want to eliminate.

From the experience gained during the COVID-19

"pandemic," they learned that fear was the best tool to get mass compliance. So they have continued to exacerbate this fear with the hoax of man-made global warming, but have made it sound friendlier to get compliance for the coming "climate lockdowns"– smiley-face tyranny. Hence the "15 Minute" cities (chapter 8). All for the greater good, of course.

The Merchants of Death, the multibillionaires club, the globalist sorcerers, the global oligarchs have, for many decades, been developing their plan to establish their *New World Order*. We cannot help but acknowledge the connections we see to the biblical prophecies, particularly the 4 horsemen of the Apocalypse (chapter 9). This is biblical. We are facing an existential threat to our survival on planet Earth.

Regardless, we need not fear the threat of the oligarchs' *New World Order*, because God has given us ample warning. He has also allowed us to recognize this as a war primarily against Him (chapter 10). Lucifer believes that he can defeat God and he has been manipulating these Merchants of Death to achieve his goals on Earth. But God has His own plans and we can count on His Son to "deliver us from the evil one". God is sovereign and to Him belongs all "the power and the glory forever and ever". The only "Great Reset" that you need is God's, and that is within the reach of us all.

1

THE GLOBAL OLIGARCHY'S NEOFASCIST AGENDA

THE WORLD ECONOMIC FORUM (WEF) IS AN international non-governmental lobbying organization established in 1971 by German engineer and economist Klaus Schwab. The Forum is headquartered in Switzerland and, since its inception, has sponsored projects that are enthusiastically embraced by those wanting to overturn the existing world economic order. Lately, the WEF has been resolutely promoting the 'Great Reset'. But what is the 'Great Reset'?

In a nutshell, the Great Reset is a totalitarian plan of the global oligarchs to 'reset' the entire world economy. This process requires ending private property and dismantling 'shareholder capitalism'. Schwab and fellow global oligarchs, including King Charles III, have been making arguments against 'shareholder capitalism' for literally decades, going all the way back to the 1970s.[1]

The COVID-19 pandemic was perceived as a great opportunity to refashion the world, weaponise the digital revolution, and "save" the planet from the effects of "climate change".

THE WEF'S proposal of a Great Reset requires not only corporate responses to pandemics and ecological issues such as "climate change", but the wholesale rethinking of corporations' duties towards "vulnerable communities within the ecosystems". To this effect, the international community has already developed the Environmental, Social, and Governance (ESG) Index to "drive ownership and control of production away from the non-woke or non-compliant."[2]

This entails the collaboration of the corporate world with big government to crush the spirit of individual liberty.

In profound ways, the fixation of the global oligarchs on a "new world order" is reminiscent of the totalitarian past. Similar to the modern globalists, the fascists of the past also aspired to create "a new society and a new man". Fascism is based on the supremacy of community over the individual, so that individual rights are entirely subordinated to the organic interests of the state. The idea is encapsulated in the famous Nazi motto, "common welfare before individual interest". Hitler expressed such a view in a speech on 7 October 1933:

> *"It is necessary that the individual should come to realize that his own ego is of no importance in comparison with the existence of his nation; that the position of the individual ego is conditioned solely by the interests of the community as a whole ... We understand only the individual's capacity to make sacrifices for the community, for his fellow man".*[3]

Are we suggesting that a person is fascist if she or he cares about the community? Of course not. However, a simple fact remains: the economic ideas of Klaus Schwab are similar to the corporatist ideologies that spawned fascist economics in the 1920s and 1930s. What is fascist about the globalist movement is the notion that, in an "organic community", the individual has no basic human rights and the government can force us to do something for our own good.

Naturally, there are different forms of fascism, but what unites them are their emotional impulses, such as the urge to "get beyond politics" coupled with a faith in the authority of experts, an obsession with the cult of "urgent action", and the need for an all-powerful state to coordinate everyone towards the achievement of an ultimate goal.

Most of all, those who embrace the globalist agenda tend to share a common belief–a totalitarian temptation–that with the right amount of governmental tinkering we can finally realize some utopian dream of "creating a better world".[4]

Curiously, according to Kaitlin Smith, a Boston-based scholar and naturalist educator, "Nazi leadership [also] ardently championed renewable energy, and institutionalized organic farming and land use planning on a level unmatched by any nation past or present".[5]

It is instructive to highlight another example of how totalitarian power can be advanced and consolidated. Nazi Germany led the world in the area of epidemiology. Nazi ideologues contrasted the notion of health as a communal duty with the notion that people could not do as they wished with their own bodies.[6]

Under the influence of Nazi ideology, medical research scientists did not repudiate the use of humans for medical experiments.[7]

With criminal law and civil liability laws conveniently suspended, medical doctors apparently thought that their actions were morally justified.

Hitler lamented, in 1925, that the State still did not have the means to "master the disease" which was penetrating the "bloodstream of our people unhindered". These ideas saw the German population as a patient of the State and the political leader as the beneficent physician.[8] The images of Jews as the carriers of a deadly disease resulted from bio-political content merged with Nazi medical science. Hence the race laws of 1935 were underpinned by images of immunity against a virus and the need for general immunization of the entire population. To further instill fear among the population, a recurrent theme in Nazi propaganda was the idea that Jews spread infectious-contagious diseases, including the dreaded typhus. Health officers produced posters with a quarantine notice at the entrance to the ghettos, warning the curious about the dangers of venturing into those spaces of segregation. Since the sanitary conditions imposed on those confined areas were deeply degrading, this created a propitious environment for the rapid spread of previously announced diseases. As a consequence, this turned the warning of Nazi authorities into a form of self-fulfilling prophecy.

Far from being limited to the recruitment of health agents, the Nazis also relied on the support of those working for the big corporations that are today often described as "Big Data" and "Big Tech". As the precursors of the digital universe we know today, the technology of old punch cards provided the Nazi regime with the data compilation required in the process of identification, tracking, confiscation, incarceration, deportation and, finally, the extermination of the "unwanted".

In addition to control of information, and complicity of the medical and scientific communities, as well as the technical support of the greatest Big Tech of the time, the Nazis also relied on the most powerful Big Pharma company of those days – the pharmaceutical conglomerate *IG Farben*. Formed in 1925 after the merger of several chemical and pharmaceutical industries, the *IG Farben* group developed a lethal gas that was used to eliminate millions of Jews in extermination camps. The company also produced other devastating gasses for military use which, were providentially never used in World War II.[9]

Unfortunately, we are witnessing today the fulfillment of the well-known statement attributed to Ronald Reagan, that freedom is only a generation away from extinction. How far are we from unleashing a new and devastating totalitarian technocracy, in the mold of the scientism experienced by the unwary Germans of the 1930s? In George Orwell's dystopian novel "1984" the *New Thought Police* were able to control the ideas that determined the political and cultural values of society. The withdrawal of personal freedoms in our present time has been sold to the populace as a positive thing and a means of protecting them from any perceived threat. Slavery to the State has been presented as the gateway to health and prosperity.

Ronnie Cummins, in his chapter entitled *How the Pandemic Plans Unfolded* (which opens the book by Dr. Joseph Mercola) is clear in stating that beyond its effects on health and the healthcare industry, COVID-19 has empowered the global elite more than ever before to manufacture lies and half-truths. Uber-powerful Silicon Valley Big Tech corporations (Facebook, Google, Microsoft, and Amazon), Big Pharma, the World Health Organization (WHO), and philanthropic giant Bill Gates have indentured politicians and scientists from across the political spectrum.

From the fight against a "pandemic" to the obsession with "sustainability", nobody disputes that these are ideas of the cultural Left. Unfortunately, only a few of us are willing to consider that we have seen these sorts of things before. Under Hitler, the dissenter risked imprisonment and death. Today, the dissenter risks the loss of the professional license and even imprisonment. Of course, the present globalist movement is committed to removing any opposition to their totalitarian agenda. If we allow their plan to be successful, the current economic system will be entirely destroyed and replaced with a centralized economic system, with a special emphasis placed on the elimination of individual rights. If you value your rights to privacy, to property, to free speech, and to democratic representation, be very wary of the 'Great Reset'. You must fight against it, before it's too late.

2

THE GLOBAL OLIGARCHS' DEATH WISH AND THE WUHAN LAB LEAK

MAO ZEDONG, THE FOUNDER OF COMMUNIST CHINA, was a faithful Marxist who supported an adaptation of a Western ideology from Vladimir Lenin. This led to the first successful Communist Revolution, in 1917 in Russia. When the Chinese Communists obtained full control over the nation, on October 1st, 1949, they created a regime closely modeled on Soviet Russia. Initially, Mao faithfully copied Stalin's economic policies, collectivizing agriculture and introducing Five-Year Plans of industrialization.

However, after the death of Stalin in 1953 Mao refused to play by the rules formulated by the Communist leadership in Soviet Russia. He regarded Stalin's successors as traitors to Marxism-Leninism and consequently he claimed himself the leader of a Marxist doctrine designed for world destruction and domination. In many of his conversations Mao poured deep scorn on his own people. When it came to the question 'How do you change China?' his answer was quite emphatic: "The country must be destroyed and then re-formed".[1]

IN 1966 MAO launched a vicious campaign directed against Chinese intellectuals and party officials. For several years China, one of the world's oldest civilizations, was ravaged by barbarian hordes who had been taught to treat everything beyond their understanding as fit for destruction. Some courageous officers begged Mao to be more merciful. They were rebuked with remarks like this: "You have too much mercy, not enough brutality, which means you are not so Marxist. On this matter", Mao added, "we indeed have no conscience! Marxism is that brutal".[2]

Mao was quite right. Socialism is an evil ideology and 'the struggle for socialism', wrote Marx, requires his disciples "to eliminate the conditions of morality and circumstances of justice".[3]

With this idea in mind Mao concluded that destroying the Chinese culture was not enough. He also had to create a "New Chinese Man".

Of course, changing humanity is the ultimate objective of Marxism. But Mao decided it had to be realized without delay, so he committed his entire rule to make it reality. He had inherited from Marx the ideas of destruction and violence as perfectly valid political strategies. With astonishing indifference to human life, on a visit to Moscow, in 1957, Mao expressed his desire to even sacrifice half of all humanity: "If worst came to the worst and half of mankind died, the other half would remain while imperialism would be razed to the ground and the whole world would become socialist".[4]

That same year, in Moscow, Mao deeply shocked his Soviet comrades with comments about a possible war against Western countries and its consequences: "We may lose more than 300 million. So what? ... The years will pass and we'll get to work producing more babies than ever before".[5]

ALTHOUGH ANYONE in China who dared to criticize Mao risked immediate imprisonment, the Western economic oligarchs and left-wing intelligentsia openly sympathized with him and sought wisdom in his insipid writings. One such admirer was David Rockefeller, the American banker and chief executive of the Chase Manhattan Corporation. Rockefeller claimed that Mao somehow had succeeded "not only in producing a more efficient and dedicated administration, but also in fostering high morale and community of purpose".[6]

Undoubtedly, Mao's administration was incredibly "efficient" in exterminating people, indeed well over 60 million Chinese people, thus killing more people than any other in the entire history of mankind.[7] In all of this, Mao received considerable support from the western oligarchs. Rockefeller notoriously stated in an August 10, 1973 article in The New York Times: "Chairman Mao's leadership is one of the most important and successful in human history".[8]

Today, Western ties with the virus lab at the Wuhan Institute of Virology are clearly demonstrated. It has been reported that the National Institute of Allergy and Infectious Diseases, headed by the American coronavirus tsar Dr. Anthony Fauci, gave millions of dollars of American taxpayers' money to the Wuhan Institute of Virology.[9] Indeed, internal emails of Fauci obtained through the Freedom of Information Act (FOIA) has cast a spotlight on the longstanding relationship between at least one American epidemiology professor and that controversial lab.[10]

Anthony Fauci served as director of the U.S. National Institute of Allergy and Infectious Diseases (NIAID) from 1984 to 2022, and as chief medical advisor to the U.S. president from 2021 to 2022. Fauci's agency funded about 60 research projects at the Wuhan laboratory.[11] "Then he even wrote a paper where he said gain-of-function research was worth the risk of a pandemic, stating that he had even funded coronavirus research in conjunction with the Chinese military", says Sharri Markson, a *Sky News Australia* journalist.[12]

Of course, it is quite undeniable that China is now far more prosperous and less overtly violent than it was under Mao. But because the regime has never fully disavowed its Founder, one may expect that it might still be prepared to return to some of Mao's original methods in difficult moments.[13]

What were then these original methods?

We should allow Mao to speak for himself: "The country must be destroyed. This also applies to mankind. ... People like me long for its destruction, because when the old is destroyed, a new universe will be formed. Isn't that better!"[14]

The Western ruling classes have been, for quite a long time, talking about population control, which is a form of totalitarian control over the world's poorest citizens. They have spoken of a "war on population growth" and used military analogies to achieve their goal. "The war would entail sacrifices and collateral damage", says Matthew Connelly, a historian of population control at Columbia University in New York.[15]

Accordingly, University of Texas ecologist Eric Pianka once told a meeting of the *Texas Academy of Science* that at least 90 per cent of his fellow human beings must die in order to "save the planet".[16]

Reflecting on the *Ancient Chinese Curse*, "May you live in interesting times," Pianka asserted: "We're looking forward to a huge collapse. Disease will control the scourge of humanity," he said. "This is really an exciting time," Pianka added amid warnings of apocalypse, destruction and disease, thus concluding: "Death. This is what awaits us all. Death."

Such a language betrays a complete lack of empathy with fellow human beings coupled with an utmost desire to bring death and destruction at a large scale. Though these statements are profoundly disturbing, Pianka is not without abundant advocates. What links this revered biologist to other equally influential members of the Western ruling classes is this: they wholeheartedly embrace the notion that dramatic reduction of the world's population is necessary to "save the planet".

Curiously, Dr. Steven Quay, who holds a master's and a doctorate degree from the University of Michigan, and Richard Muller, an emeritus professor of physics at the University of California-Berkeley, suggest a lab origin regarding the outbreak of COVID-19. In fact, Professor Muller is entirely convinced that COVID-19 is "a million-to-one proposition to have arisen naturally". He goes on to say that it is "extremely likely" that the virus was deliberately created in that notorious lab at the *Wuhan Institute of Virology*.[17]

Dr. Robert Redfield, the former director of U.S. Centers for Disease Control and Prevention (CDC), is equally convinced that COVID-19 originated in that Chinese lab which was sponsored by that American governmental agency.[18] On September 16, 2020, he told members of the U.S. Senate Appropriations Subcommittee on Labor, Health and Human Services, Education and Related Agencies, that "gain-of-function research, which involves manipulating the virus to make it become more infectious in lab environments, was likely being funded by U.S. agencies at the Wuhan Institute".[19] While explaining that he opposes gain-of-function research, as "such acts involve manipulating the virus to make it become more infectious in lab environments", Dr.Redfield went on to state that "it was highly likely that U.S. agencies funded such research at the Wuhan Institute".[20]

Curiously, one year before the outbreak of the bioengineered virus, research scientists at the Wuhan lab submitted a detailed research plan to the U.S. Defense

Advanced Research Project Agency (DARPA) to create a "Frankenstein coronavirus". [21]

These researchers reported virus sequences to the National Institutes of Health (NIH), a part of the U.S. Department of Health and Human Services, but then called in June 2020 to ask for that information to be deleted, a request that was honored by the NIH.

It is almost impossible to discredit the persuasive theory that COVID-19 did not simply "escape" from the Wuhan lab. This theory is further justified by the fact that a key Chinese scientist who collaborated with the Wuhan Institute of Virology, Dr. Zhou Yusen, filed for a patent for a COVID-19 vaccine on February 24, 2020. Yet, less than three months after filling his patent, he "died under mysterious circumstances". The early timing of his filing of that vaccine patent further raises the suspicion that the "pandemic" was the result of a deliberate leak of the novel coronavirus.

Of course, COVID-19 pandemic has conveniently facilitated an authoritarian decision-making environment and created an unsustainable welfare state while crushing the independent sectors of the global economy. Hence, snitching, suppression of free speech, artificial intelligence and facial recognition technologies, government-sanctioned discrimination against the unvaccinated, and the allocation of a social credit score have been used to facilitate the advent of a *new world order* by the global oligarchs.

3

MAN-MADE GLOBAL FAMINE

"YOU WILL OWN NOTHING, AND YOU WILL BE STARVING!"

THE GLOBAL OLIGARCHS HAVE BEEN BUSY undermining food security for decades. Food security is what these oligarchs, led by the World Economic Forum (WEF), intend to destroy, so they can impose a new food system based on patented, ultra-processed foods, meat substitutes and "green" protein alternatives such as cricket meal and mealworms. According to Dr. Joseph Mercola, an osteopathic physician and recipient of multiple awards in the field of natural health,

> "The end goal of The Great Reset-pushing elitists is to own everything and control the entire global population through a combination of false flag disasters, social engineering technologies, "green" and "sustainable" development policies, a revamped food system of their own making, and global security measures".[1]

These oligarchs are now admonishing us of a possible global famine that may be caused by extraordinary human conflicts and natural disasters. For example, the Dutch government has recently released a statement which attempts to deflect the attention of the general public from their own extreme anti-farming policies by claiming that "because of climate change, poor harvests, armed conflicts and population growth, the danger of famine is increasing".[2]

The Netherlands, a tiny country in terms of land and population, is nevertheless the second largest food exporter in the world, after the United States, a country much larger in territory and with around 20 times the population.[3] This is all soon coming to an end because the Dutch farmers complain that their property rights have been seriously undermined by legislation that threatens agricultural undertakings with elimination.

It is estimated that up to 3,000 farmers will have to close down their productive farms due to governmental policies which effectively blame them for "high greenhouse emissions", despite the nation contributing with only 5.2 per cent of all the EU emissions.[4]

Writing for *The Spectator Australia*, Xin Du comments:

> *"The Dutch policies are particularly puzzling, as Dutch farmers are among the most efficient in the world … It is therefore mind-boggling that the Dutch government and the EU would want to uproot this industry rather than to promote and emulate it in a world that is running out of food".*[5]

Of course, "running out of food" is not something that occurs at random or cannot be avoided. Many countries including Canada, Germany and Sri Lanka are following a similar agenda to undermine the agricultural sector by reducing nitrogen in the environment by at least 30 per cent. Joshua Phillip, an investigative reporter and recognised expert on asymmetrical hybrid warfare, says "the nitrogen reduction policies and chemical fertilizer trends in the majority of countries around the world will lead to food shortages, like what happened in Sri Lanka recently".[6]

In the Spring of 2021, President Rajapaksa of the Sri Lankan government banned the importation of synthetic fertilizers and pesticides forcing the farmers to convert to organic farming, essentially "overnight". Food production collapsed and the economy went into free fall.

"Runaway inflation reached 54.6 percent last month, and the South Asian country is now headed toward bankruptcy. Nine in 10 Sri Lankan families are skipping meals, and many are standing in line for days in the hope of acquiring fuel.

"The agrochemical ban caused rice production to drop 20 percent in the six months after it was implemented, causing a country that had been self-sufficient in rice production to spend $450 million on rice imports — much more than the $400 million that would've been saved by banning fertilizer imports.

"The production of tea, Sri Lanka's literal cash crop — it's the country's biggest export — fell by 18 percent. The government has had to spend hundreds of millions on subsidies and compensation to farmers in an effort to make up for the loss of productivity." [7]

What is the real agenda behind all of this? Though we do not support the use of pesticides on agricultural products, the suddenness of the president's edict caused the disaster. But why was it introduced? Just look to the United Nations (UN) and its insane environmental and sustainability agenda. It is the propaganda of overpopulation and environmental damage that leads governments like these to implement such rash, insane programs.

WE ARE NOW BEING TOLD that producing food is bad for the planet. Therefore to "save the planet", the globalist cabal insists that farming must be shut down across the globe.

"Under the guise of reducing "methane emissions," thirteen nations have signed a pledge to engineer global famine by gutting agricultural production and shutting down farms. Announced earlier this year by the Global Methane Hub.[8]*-- a cabal of crisis engineers who exploit public panic to destroy the world food supply -- those thirteen nations are:*

Argentina, Australia, Brazil, Burkina Faso, Chile, Czech Republic, Ecuador, Germany, Panama, Peru, Spain, the United States, and Uruguay."[9]

"You will own nothing, and you will be happy." This confronting statement emanates from the *World Economic Forum* (WEF), a non-governmental organization established in 1971 by Klaus Schwab. By all appearances, the WEF is the most powerful organization in the world. For decades, it has been at the center of bringing together the world's richest and most powerful in business and politics. In 2006, the WEF's founder and chairman, Klaus Schwab, was knighted by Queen Elizabeth II as 'Knight Commander of the Order of Saint Michael and Saint George' (KCMG).[10]

The World Economic Forum has become the driving force in the world especially after COVID-19. In July 2020, Schwab co-authored and published a book entitled 'COVID-19: The Great Reset'. With this publication, he sought to identify the weaknesses of the present economic system which, according to him, were exposed by the alleged pandemic. Schwab's WEF considers COVID-19 as a "rare but narrow window of opportunity" to reset the global economy.[11] This involves the elimination of national borders and the removal of property rights and, indeed, any other individual right from the rest of us. In what is perhaps even more remarkable, the Great Reset also involves changing human beings. According to political economist and financial journalist James Gorrie,

> *"Schwab's WEF cohort is professor and author Yuval Noah Harari, who has publicly declared that free will in human beings is "over" and that humans are just "hackable animals" to be controlled by digital or nanochip implants. According to Schwab, under the Forth Industrial Revolution, humans will be genetically altered and chipped in the fusion of digital technology and human beings"*.[12]

Above all, the primary goal of the Great Reset is to restructure the entire world into a top-down dictatorship that is ruled by the global oligarchy. "COVID-19 restrictions and measures to tackle climate change are pillars of the Great Reset initiative aimed to remake global capitalism, leading ultimately to tyrannical control over societies", says climate journalist and political aide Marc Morano.[13]

The cult of environmentalism, ferociously promoted by the UN/WEF oligarchs, constitutes a major cause of famine now and into the future. The globalists claim nitrous oxide is a greenhouse gas and we must stop meat production to reduce it. This is just another scam of the global warming cultists. The truth of the matter is that the globalists want the land to build a new green city with thousands of hectares of solar farms to power their futuristic wet-dream city. So, how is that going to affect global food supplies? Not very well we suspect.

We have seen this in Brazil when the former President Jair Bolsonaro tried to import synthetic fertilizer from Russia. Brazil is the world's fourth largest food producer and it needs a steady supply of fertilizers to power its impressive agricultural industry. [14]

And yet, the country's largest international supplier of

fertilizers is precisely Russia, which accounts for 44 per cent of the total the country consumes each year, making it the world's largest importer of fertilizers.[15]

When the war in Ukraine broke out the Brazilian President was intelligent enough to ignore globalist demands and meet with Vladimir Putin in Moscow, on 16 February 2022, to reassure continuing cooperation between both countries in various fields, including agriculture.[16]

Above all, Brazil desperately needed to import 97 per cent of the roughly 10 million tonnes of potassium it uses for crop production each year, thus making it the world's largest importer.[17]

As one may expect, Bolsonaro's visit to Russia was heavily criticized by the U.S. government. Thankfully, the Brazilian leader did not back down and an agreement with Russia was made that objectively saved the world from a catastrophic food crisis. "If Brazil were to scale back next year because of a lack of fertilizer, that would certainly be bad news for a global food crisis", says Joseph Schmidhuber, an economist who has studied the conflict's impact on food for the UN Food and Agriculture Organization.[18]

The world should therefore be most grateful to Bolsonaro but unfortunately he was not re-elected in the presidential elections held in November of 2022. The U.S. Government did absolutely everything at its disposal to actually remove him from the presidential office in Brazil. U.S. President Joe Biden effectively orchestrated a ferocious international campaign against his re-election.[19]

If there is anything COVID-19 has taught us it is that many governments are not working for the people. To the contrary, these governments are following the script of the WEF's Great Reset, which "is tied to the climate change and the green new deal policies pushed in the United States, Europe and some other countries as well as the United Nations' climate agenda and net-zero initiative".[20]

The WEF recommendation to "build back better" has been adopted in the United States as a "climate change policy".[21] In that country, farmers no longer can find enough chemical nitrogen fertilizer to grow their crops.[22] Under the Biden administration, this too has led to the collapse of the current energy system in order to lower carbon dioxide emissions. [23]

The US Department of Agriculture (USDA) recently released a disturbing report that essentially warns the American public about inevitable food shortages.[24] The threat of food shortage in that country has been further aggravated by governmental policies that result in rising interest rates, price inflation, and excessive environmental regulations that, when combined, create very serious problems for that nation's agrarian and livestock sector.[25]

It is the WEF's propaganda of overpopulation and environmental damage that leads governments to implement such rash, insane policies. How is that going to affect global food supplies? Not very well we suspect. How do you reduce the global demand on resources and limit environmental damage? Depopulate the world of humans.

We are constantly told that there are too many people on this planet and it can't support them all. Of course, concerns about population growth are not new and, in 1968, ecologist Paul Ehrlich predicted worldwide famine due to overpopulation. "Sometime in the next 15 years, the end will come", Ehrlich told CBS News in a prophetic tone. [26] Needless to say these apocalyptic predictions about catastrophic overpopulation have proved to be entirely false over and over again.[27] In spite of all the worry, access to food and resources increased as population rose.[28]

The World Economic Forum agreed about implementing

the Club of Rome's agenda of dramatic world depopulation. This has been the program of the Club of Rome, an oligarchical think-tank, as far back as 1972 when its members were concerned with global resources and overpopulation. Renowned primatologist Jane Goodall said, at the World Economic Forum (WEF) in 2020:

> *"We cannot hide away from human population growth, because it underlies so many of the other problems. All these [environmental] things we talk about wouldn't be a problem if the world was the size of the population that there was 500 years ago."* [29]

In 1600, the world population is estimated to have been 500 to 580 million. [30] That means 94 percent less humans in the world! We are meant to believe that reducing the world's population to 500 million will relieve the environment of the stress on both resources and environmental damage. According to James Tonkowich, a scholar at the *Institute on Religion & Democracy* in Washington, D.C., there is indeed a long history of environmentalist thinking that sees humans primarily as consumers and polluters. [31] Interestingly, somehow we are meant to believe that reducing the world's population by 94 percent will change the weather. This has been the program of the *Club of Rome* as far back as 1972 when its first report *"Limits to Growth"* stated,

> *"With no major change in the physical, economic or social relationships that have traditionally governed world development, society will run out of the non-renewable resources in 100 years".*

Curiously, biologist Eric Pianka, the "Texas Distinguished Scientist of 2006", contended in the 1992 proceedings of the *Texas Academy of Science* that, in order to "save the planet", the size of the world's population should be reduced by 90 per cent. Forrest Mims, Chairman of the Environmental Science Section of the Texas Academy of Science, writing at *The Citizen Scientist*, comments on the "final solution" proposed by him:

"Professor Pianka said the Earth as we know it will not survive without drastic measures. Then, and without presenting any data to justify this number, he asserted that the only feasible solution to saving the Earth is to reduce the population to 10 percent of the present number.

"He then showed solutions for reducing the world's population in the form of a slide depicting the Four Horsemen of the Apocalypse. War and famine would not do, he explained. Instead, disease offered the most efficient and fastest way to kill the billions that must soon die if the population crisis is to be solved... AIDS is not an efficient killer, he explained, because it is too slow. His favorite candidate for eliminating 90 percent of the world's population is airborne Ebola (Ebola Reston), because it is both highly lethal and it kills in days, instead of years.

"After praising the Ebola virus for its efficiency at killing, Pianka paused, leaned over the lectern, looked at us and carefully said, We've got airborne 90 percent mortality in humans. Killing humans. Think about that." [32]

The oligarchical plan of massive human depopulation can be done, and has been done, through engineered wars. In the First World War 21.5 million died of which 13 million were civilians. The civilian deaths were largely caused by starvation, exposure, disease, military encounters and massacres. In the Second World War, 40-50 million died, the largest of any war. [33]

Then there were the massacres by the communists. For example, Joseph Stalin's Bolsheviks (1929-53) killed 40-60 million in the former Soviet Union, and Mao Zedong's communist regime (1946-76) killed 65-78 million in China. [34]

The war in Ukraine, coupled with the West's economic

sanctions, has put the world's food security at tremendous risk. These sanctions are supposedly meant to punish Russia for its invasion of Ukraine. However, they are causing a serious danger to the world's ability to feed itself.[35] In the worst-case scenario, says Chris Barrett, an agricultural economist at Cornell University, "we are going to see tens of millions of people suddenly facing famine".[36]

We are presently experiencing an asymmetric war, partially kinetic (NATO/Ukraine vs. Russia), but primarily a silent war whereby food shortages are engineered. This is achieved through shutting down production by driving farmers from the land, banning live animal exports, and disrupting supply lines like we saw in the "pandemic" years.

But probably the greatest driver of famine is none of the above, but in fact the supply of currency and credit. Control the food supply and you control the people; but control the money supply and you control the whole world. Of course, controlling the money supply also directly affects the food supply. We may very soon experience a reality of apocalyptic proportions. Curiously, in the book of Revelation, Chapter 6, verses 5 and 6, we read:

"I looked, and there before me was a black horse! Its rider was holding a pair of scales in his hand. Then I heard what sounded like a voice ...,
saying, "Two pounds of wheat for a day's wages, and six pounds of
barley for a day's wages, and do not damage the oil and the wine!"

This is one of the 4 horsemen of the Apocalypse which brings famine. Black is the color of mourning. The scales indicate that the land was torn by engineered economic war, and is filled with sorrow, mourning and despair. This includes sanctions and control of global credit, which has been happening for a long time, and the populace is diverted by talk of price inflation being the cause of high food prices. But that is putting the cart before the horse (no pun intended). Fiat currency printing is the most important cause of price inflation as the value of the dollar deflates.

It goes without saying that since 2008 the world-dominating US Federal Reserve has been "printing money" like never before. Currently, the amount is already 2.3 times larger (in the same dollar terms) than was "printed" during and after World War II and there is no stopping. [37] Since the US dollar is the global reserve currency, either hyperinflation will result and/or a total global economic collapse will ensue. Either way, it doesn't matter, global famine will accelerate. It is inevitable.

We need to wake up to these tactics of the global oligarchs and resist all efforts to impose their dystopian objectives on us. We need to stop the wasteful kinetic wars and stop the war on citizens by insane fiat currency printing. Above all, we must stop the woke depopulation agenda and put an end to the WEF's ungodly fascist agenda before it is actually too late. Otherwise, paraphrasing WEF's statement, "you will own nothing and you will be starving!"

4

PUSHING HARD FOR WORLD WAR III

Why do wars start? Do they start without provocation? Are wars avoidable? The scripture in James 4:1-2 provides a good answer: *"...come they not hence, even of your lusts ... you kill, and desire to have, and cannot obtain: you fight and war..."*

Wars are not the result of random chance. Deliberate planning and provocation are involved and often an excuse is evoked for countries to declare war on another. Currently, we are seeing the advanced stages of just this as the US and its NATO allies have been maneuvering for many years for a world war with Russia. They yell that it is to protect "freedom and democracy" as they conquer and extort the wealth of the conquered nation as well as that of the conquering nations.

Lust or desire to take resources from another nation is the cause of war. Those resources include oil, gas, minerals, gold and the souls of men (slaves). But there is more to it than that.

"War, Boom, Bust" is often heard in the context of economic cycles in history. A war is needed to get a country or empire out of the doldrums of the last economic bust. The manufacturing industry building war machinery is turned on and that fuels the economy, driving enormous "boom" activity, which gives the illusion and also the reality of prosperity, at least temporarily.

A small number of industrialists and banksters become extremely rich. But the boom is only a veneer, because war never builds a society, it only destroys, and the boom does not last. It always comes crashing to an end. Inevitably, as the war machine comes to a halt we get the next "bust" in the cycle, a depression which can last for many years.

You can look back thousands of years and you will see the tendency to deface the money of the realm to finance wars. The Romans melted down their pure silver or gold coins and added base metals to expand the currency supply. The more base metals, like copper, were added the more the real money was deflated.

After the printing press was invented paper currency could easily be printed. This saw extreme periods of "money" printing and hyperinflation. Assignats were paper money (fiat currency) issued by the Constituent Assembly in France from 1789 to 1796, during the French Revolution. They were printed to address imminent bankruptcy of the state. But it only led to more and more fiat currency printing and massive price hyperinflation.[1]

The world since 1900 has experienced two major world encompassing wars. Wars cost a lot of money and countries, even if they were initially on a gold standard, usually start massive money printing to finance their wars. This fact can be seen in the US Federal Reserve (FED) liabilities, for which data is available, from the time of their inception in 1914, just before the beginning of World War 1 (WWI).[2]

If we look at the FED liabilities taken from its published reports, and if we normalize those dollars to 1914 dollars, then we get the following chart. The normalization was achieved using the FED M2 money supply data for the years between 1959 and 2023. [3] This means we are truly comparing "apples with apples". [4]

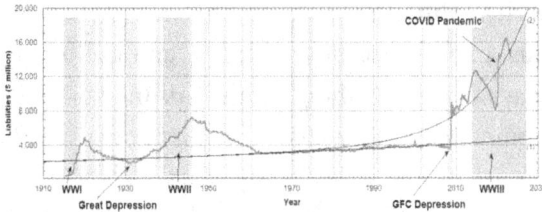

Chart 1: U.S. Federal Reserve Liabilities on its balance sheet normalized to 1914 dollars (red curve). A curve fit to the data between 1965 and 2003 is the solid trend line (1). A double exponential curve fit to the data above 2003 is the solid line (2). The World Wars are indicated by arrows pointing to the dark gray (pink) regions. Recessions are indicated by light gray (sepia) colored strips.

Chart 1 indicates that due to the massive war spending FED liabilities expanded significantly up to 1920 and then to 1946 after which they were contracted in the post war periods. The triangle shaped humps above the trend line (1) and labeled WWI and WWII indicate this fact. But between these periods of massive money printing was the Great Depression of 1930-32. The FED liabilities dipped below the trend line (1) then.

Now looking to the period after 2000 we see again the liabilities dipped below the trend line and indicate the depression brought on by sub-prime mortgages in the Global Financial Crisis (GFC). After this the FED massively began expanding its liabilities. It roughly follows the exponential growth indicated by trend line (2).

In 2014 the FED began again contracting its liabilities until 2020 when the COVID-19 pandemic started. Is it a coincidence that the Russia-Ukraine war also started in early 2014 in the

Donbas region of the country after the overthrow of the democratically elected government of President Victor Yanukovych via a U.S. backed coup? For this reason we have drawn the start of a potential new world war (WWIII) from that time on Chart 1.

It is instructive to ascertain what happened to Ukraine in 2014. It revolves around a coup supported by the U.S. government. With the victory of Viktor Yanukovych in the presidential elections of 2010, the Ukrainian Parliament voted to abandon NATO membership aspirations.[5] Perhaps precisely because of this, Yanukovych was unconstitutionally ousted in February 2014 in an U.S.-backed coup.[6]

Article 108 of the Ukrainian Constitution lists four circumstances in which an elected president may cease to exercise power before the end of their term: retirement; inability to exercise their powers for reasons of health; removal from office by the procedure of impeachment; and death.

The process of impeachment is laid down in Article 111, which requires the Ukrainian Parliament to create a special temporary investigation committee to formulate charges against the president, seek evidence to justify the charges, and come to conclusions about the president's guilt. Prior to a final vote of impeachment, this process also requires the nation's Constitutional Court to review the case and certify that the procedure has been properly followed, and the Ukrainian Supreme Court to certify that the acts of which the President is accused are worthy of impeachment. Finally, the removal of an elected president in Ukraine must be approved by at least three-quarters of the members of Parliament.

On February 22, 2014, this process of impeachment was not followed at all. No investigation committee was formed, and no courts were involved in the removal of the President. Instead, a bill was rushed through the Ukrainian Parliament to remove Yanukovych from his office, although this was not even supported by the three-quarters of Members of Parliament, as required by Article 111.

Ever since that coup Ukraine has never been able to have a functional government. Russia almost immediately retaliated by annexing the Crimea, in March 2014. Crimeans, who mostly speak Russian, voted overwhelmingly to join the Russian Federation. Writing for the *American Conservative*, foreign policy expert Dominick Sansone comments:

> *"The move into Crimea came as a response, to secure Russia's key naval interests in the warm-water port at Sevastopol. The coinciding uprisings in the Donbas were additionally a response to the situation in Kiev ... The official position of the Kremlin has subsequently been that these ethnically Russian citizens should not be forced to live under the rule of an illegitimate rebel group that illegally came to power by overthrowing the duly elected government".* [7]

The reality is that the eastward expansion of NATO is what has triggered the war in Ukraine, primarily due to Washington's attempt to pull Ukraine into its orbit and defense structure by building an explicitly anti-Moscow association and supporting a notoriously corrupt and oppressive regime in Kyiv.[8] "With regards to Ukraine", writes Professor John Mearsheimer, an American political scientist and international relations scholar,

> *"It's very important to understand that, up until 2014, we did not envision NATO expansion and E.U. expansion as a policy that was aimed at containing Russia. Nobody seriously thought that Russia was a threat before February 22, 2014. What happened is that this major crisis broke out, and we had to assign blame, and of course we were never going to blame ourselves. We were going to blame the Russians so*

we invented this story that Russia was bent on aggression in Eastern Europe".[9]

The rationale for the creation of NATO was that it would be a defensive alliance to stop the former Soviet Union from invading Western Europe. However, when the Soviet Union collapsed in the late 1980s, if its claims were truthful this organization would have been dismantled, its purported purpose now moot. Instead, since the mid-1990s successive U.S. administrations have regularly pushed for NATO expansion in Eastern Europe.[10] The Czech Republic, Hungary, and Poland joined the Alliance in March 1999. Five years later, Bulgaria, Romania, Latvia, Lithuania and Estonia also joined the Alliance. Then, in an April 2008 summit in Bucharest, NATO considered admitting Georgia and Ukraine, which the Russians maintained would represent a "direct threat" to their national security.[11]

The Russians saw this as a betrayal of a promise made by the U.S. government on the collapse of the Berlin Wall that NATO would never advance "even one inch to the east". This present crisis in Ukraine is primarily the result of an attempt by the U.S. government to pull another Eastern European country decisively into its orbit and defense structure, via NATO membership/partnership and an explicitly anti-Moscow E.U. association agreement.[12]

Article 5 in NATO's founding document states that any armed attack against any member of the alliance "shall be considered an attack against them all". Ukraine is now a "close partner" of NATO, which reports providing "unprecedented levels" of military support to its government.[13] To date, NATO member countries have provided billions of euros' worth of military equipment to Ukraine".[14] They are sending weapons, ammunition and many types of light and heavy military equipment, including anti-tank and anti-air systems, howitzers and drones. "Since 2014", NATO's official website states,

> "NATO has helped to reform Ukraine's armed forces and defence institutions, including with equipment and financial support. Allies have also provided training for tens of thousands of Ukrainian troops and Ukrainian forces have also developed their capabilities by participation in NATO exercises and operations".[15]

Ukraine is a multi-ethnic nation and many Ukrainians are ethnic Russians. Don't Russian-speaking Ukrainians have a right to celebrate their own culture and heritage? Apparently not. Under the pro-U.S. regime of Volodymyr Zelensky, Ukraine has enacted a series of laws aimed at the so-called "de-russification" of Ukraine.[16] Russian books and even Russian music have been banned by the Zelensky regime.[17] Only books published in Ukrainian or "the indigenous languages of the European Union" can now be published in Ukraine.[18]

Zelensky was the most unlikely candidate to win the 2019 Ukrainian presidential election.[19] He says that Canada's Prime Minister Justin Trudeau was "one of those leaders who inspired him" to join politics.[20] Zelensky is an acolyte of Klaus Schwab's *World Economic Forum* (WEF), the organization behind the "Great Reset", an international-socialist plan to "reset" the world economy, "and install a centralized, and heavily regulated totalitarian international system similar to that of China's Social Credit System".[21] According to Leon Kushner, a journalist who was raised by Holocaust survivors from Ukraine,

> "Ukraine is ... as corrupt as Russia or perhaps more so. Since 2014 oligarchs run it mob style and chose the then actor Zelensky to be their presidential puppet. The WEF's Klaus Schwab bragged about helping

elect him and his equivalent Canadian puppet Trudeau. Just about every rich and famous player has been to Ukraine. And came back with even more money. From Bill Gates to Joe Biden, from George Soros to the Clintons. They all know that Ukraine is open for business."[22]

On March 20, 2023, the Zelensky regime banned all the Ukrainian opposition parties, accusing its leaders of putting "their own ambitions and careers above the interests of the State". [23] He has enacted a decree that nationalizes all the private TV channels into one state-controlled platform, citing his own martial law as an excuse.[24] According to the presidential press release, this is a move to suppress so-called "active dissemination of information" and "distortion of information", namely information that is not officially endorsed by the authoritarian regime.[25]

Is this the sort of "democracy" worthy of support? The European Commission, the executive arm of the European Union, has recently announced its desire to "recommend that Ukraine be given the perspective to become a member of the European Union".[26]

Due to funds being used to support the Zelensky regime, Europe's economies are rapidly deteriorating and living standards are plummeting.[27] Europe is now facing a record depreciation of the euro currency when compared to the past 20 years.[28] A considerable number of European companies are on the verge of bankruptcy. Following catastrophic electricity and heating bills, Europe's population is facing mass unemployment and a dramatic decline in living standards.

In the United Kingdom, 60 percent of all enterprises are on the verge of closing due to higher electricity prices. Thirteen percent of British factories have reduced their working hours and 7 percent of all these factories are temporarily closed down. Electricity bills have risen by more than 100 per cent over the last two years.[29] The natural consequence will be mass business closures and rising unemployment in that country. And the Germans are equally unable to avoid recession. According to the Leibniz Institute for Economic Research, the number of firms that went bankrupt in August last year alone rose 26 percent compared to the same period in the previous year.[30]

The leading indicators show significantly higher insolvency figures, which could be around a third higher than last year.[31] "A German crisis would be a crisis for all of Europe, one that would rock the entire European Union and the many economies that surround it", says Weimin Chen, a research assistant at the Austrian Economics Center.[32]

In the United States, Steve Forbes, chairman and editor-in-chief of Forbes magazine, argues that his country is also facing a recession "making people poorer".[33] According to Nouriel Roubini, emeritus professor of economics at the New York University, it is "delusional" to expect a "short and mild" recession rather one that will be "long and severe".[34] Of course, the war in Ukraine serves to deflect the attention of the American people from domestic problems including inflation hitting its historical benchmark, the worst crime wave in U.S. history, and in Afghanistan the worst retreat in U.S. military history.[35]

Australia is also experiencing a serious cost-of-living crisis. Prices are increasing much faster than wages, which are not much higher than in 2013. In addition to the substantial increase in the price of groceries and petrol, the cost of energy has now become prohibitively high. The present energy crisis is the culmination of a global gas shortage, high coal prices and aging coal-fired power stations, as well as an irresponsible transition to unreliable "renewable" energy.

Moreover, in the midst of a serious energy crisis and the

soaring cost of living, Prime Minister Anthony Albanese announced that Australia has to achieve net-zero emissions by 2050. Speaking online on June 17, 2022 at a global economic forum convened by U.S. President Joe Biden, Albanese told other leaders that he will make sure Australia becomes a "clean energy superpower" regardless of the costs involved. He said the move would see 82 percent of Australia's National Energy market coming from renewable sources by the end of this decade. His promise is a recipe for disaster, and it certainly increases the possibility of massive blackouts in the near future. Such a possibility has already provoked an economic malaise in Australia and, indeed, throughout the Western world.

The Australian Government has deployed a formidable number of lethal weapons to Ukraine, including missiles and heavy ammunition.[36] This includes 28 Rheinmetall armored trucks, 28 M113 armored vehicles, 14 special operations vehicles, and artillery ammunition.[37] The diversion of weapons and the provision of aid to Ukraine has decisively contributed to the supply chain disruption, and the West's stifling sanctions on Russia have slowed down the recovery of the sluggish economy.

On June 26, 2023, the Australian Prime Minister announced that his country will "continue to support the war effort as long as necessary". "We will continue to work collaboratively with our partners, we are continuing to train Ukrainian forces in the United Kingdom, and we'll continue to engage with Ukraine for as long as it takes to support President Zelensky", he said.[38] But who is the idolized President of Ukraine, and why does his Ukraine deserve so much unconditional support from the Australian Prime Minister?

THE UKRAINE WAR has joined climate change and COVID-19 pandemic as the latest wellspring of government propaganda misinformation. Unfortunately, the desire to manipulate the public has become insatiable. Nobody seems to care that blatant misinformation that can lead to disastrous consequences for the world has become so prevalent. As correctly stated by journalist Adam Creighton, "It's no coincidence climate change, COVID-19 and war propaganda all have the same side-effect of increasing government power over the economy and society, and enriching a handful of powerful corporations that hold much sway over their politics, be they in pharmaceuticals, energy, or weapons manufacturing".[39]

Ukraine is notoriously identified as one of the most corrupt countries in the world and certainly the most corrupt in Europe.[40] In 2014, Ukraine was the scene of a color revolution that was sponsored by globalist organizations such as George Soros's Open Society and Klaus Schwab's WEF.[41] Ever since, Ukraine has also become the world's most popular money laundering state.[42] Then, after COVID, along came the war in Ukraine on February 24, 2022, and the leader of the most corrupt country on the continent was suddenly given "hero" status.[43]

Curiously, Schwab has bragged about helping to elect Zelensky,[44] whose government is known not only for banning political parties and closing every media outlet, except the government's propaganda agency, but also for cracking down on leaders of the Ukrainian Orthodox Church.[45] Since last year the Zelensky regime has been carrying out raids on churches and arresting their clerics on accusations of treason. In an open letter dated April 12 to Patriarch Bartholomew of Constantinople, Sylvester, vicar of the Kyiv Metropoly and rector of the Kyiv Theological Academy and Seminary, declared that this state-sponsored violence is taking place with the effective support of law enforcement authorities. According to him,

"The right to freedom of conscience and religious beliefs is being openly violated in Ukraine. It is quite obvious since the end of 2022, the Ukrainian state has set a course for the gradual destruction of the Ukrainian Orthodox Church".[46]

The Eastern Orthodox Church is the world's second largest Christian denomination, with approximately 220 million baptized members. As one of the oldest surviving religious institutions in the world, the Orthodox Church has played a prominent role in the history and culture of Eastern Europe. In Ukraine, the canonical Orthodox Church calls itself the Ukrainian Orthodox Church (UOC). In May 1992, the heads of all Orthodox Churches, including Constantinople and the Greek Church, emphasized the recognition of UOC as "the only Church that was canonical and independent in its administration of the territory of the newly created state of Ukraine".[47]

The majority of Christians in Ukraine are UOC members, especially those who live in eastern Ukraine. This persecution of Orthodox Christians in Ukraine continues to gain momentum. Of course, we should not be surprised when state-sponsored soldiers in the Ukrainian capital seize churches and monasteries, assault priests and monks of the canonical Orthodox Church, and forcibly install the members of the new pro-government sect in the holy places.[48] The Zelensky regime is notoriously hostile to Christianity and it openly supports not only abortion-on-demand and transgenderism, but also the strange phenomenon of the LGBTIQ+ soldiers who are willing to fight against Russia.[49]

Is this the sort of "democracy" worthy of Australia's support? The answer from the country's political class is a resounding yes. Australia's total support for the Ukrainian government has now climbed to A$790 million (US$520 million).[50] This is the biggest contribution by a non-NATO nation, and more support than offered by some 30 nations who are actually members of the 32-country grouping devoted to Europe's defense.[51] Of course, if the goal was to prevent further bloodshed, well, this is not the way to do it. Instead, Australia has tacitly declared war on a nuclear superpower by sending millions of dollars to the corrupt Zelensky regime as well as military equipment to Ukraine's war effort.[52]

The consequences of providing financial and military support to the Zelensky regime, as well as engaging in passionate displays of affection for the leftist dictator of that country, are deeply insensitive to the millions of Ukrainians suffering from the war and religious persecution. The European Commission, the executive arm of the European Union, has even announced its desire to "recommend that Ukraine be given the perspective to become a member of the European Union".[53] How long will these so-called "western democracies" continue 'standing for Ukraine' and be willing to suffer crippling shortages of oil and gas, as well as spiraling inflation, soaring electricity bills, food shortages and massive unemployment?

Considering all of the above, let's again look at Chart 1. If we take the real value of the expansion of the FED liabilities between 1934 and 1963 due to World War II (WWII) and compare to the total liabilities from 2008 to 2023 we find it is 2.3 times larger at its peak than in the case of WWII.

Couple this with the GFC depression from 2004 to 2008 just before the massive currency printing started in 2009 (i.e.

quantitative easing QE1 followed by QE2, QE3 and QE4)[54], does it indicate that we are already in World War III?

A comparison with previous wars, World War I (WWI) and World War II (WWII), indicates also that the FED started shrinking its balance sheet after the war was over, which makes a lot of sense, when the demand for war munitions and other wartime supplies is no longer needed. Do we have the equivalent situation now?

The FED has been aggressively expanding its balance sheet from 2020 after a period of quantitative tightening (QT) from 2014 to 2019. But that latter QT was only because of the massive expansion under QE1 to QE3. The second trend line (an exponential) fit to the data above 2003 is indicated by the solid line (2). From this we see that the periods of QT have brought the FED liabilities down to just touch this trend line (2). It is hard to see on this scale but the monetary easing used to bail out Silicon Valley Bank (SVB), Signature Bank and the other banks in March 2023 also brought the liabilities up to this trend line (2) briefly before QT continued.

It seems that the FED should be tightening (QT) and pulling its liabilities down to get back to trend line (1) yet it is expanding (QE) in an upward exponential fashion along trend line (2). Our question really is, following history: can we only expect aggressive QT to occur after the next world war ended?

Currently, the news are that the NATO/Ukrainian war with Russia is being expanded. Biden has ostensibly sent hundreds of billions of dollars in military assistance to Ukraine already. Many of the European NATO countries are joining in supplying arms and money, as has Australia. The massive Ukraine war expenditures are a big part of this current phase of quantitative easing.

The rhetoric is constantly being increased. Therefore, it would seem that this kinetic war needs to end before the FED liabilities can be contracted back down to the trend line (1) indicated in Chart 1. When will that happen? We don't know; perhaps we can ask Biden. Or whoever is running him.

A round of massive QT, with much higher bank savings rates, could do it, but with the concomitant price inflation caused by all the massive QEs after 2009, it would bring the world to financial Armageddon. You can see from the chart that the only way out for the FED is to bring their balance sheet liabilities back down to the 1963 to 2003 trend line (1). But at what cost? More bank runs and bank collapses happened in March this year (2023). However, it would seem that a kinetic World War III is inevitable if past wars are our teacher.

5
SAVE THE PLANET, SACRIFICE YOUR CHILD!

HISTORY TEACHES US THAT SOME ANCIENT civilizations killed their children to change the weather. They used to practice child sacrifice in an attempt to appease their gods and court their good graces. Those primitive peoples believed that through human sacrifice the forces of nature could be coerced in their favor. For example, the ancient Aztecs honored their gods by killing people in a field with arrows so that their blood might fertilize the land. As another example, writing for *The Spectator Australia* Alexandra Marshall explains that,

> "Half a millennia ago, the people of Chimú in northern Peru killed hundreds of children between 4-14 years old and buried them beneath the bodies of llamas in history's largest known sacrificial event. There is evidence they were brutalized first, including the removal of their hearts. The Inca weren't much better, killing children atop volcanos in Pichu Pichu and Ampato where it is believed they were tied to stone slabs and left to be struck by lightning".[1]

We may be just repeating history. The modern environmental movement can be compared to a pantheistic religion. It certainly contains a vision of sin and repentance, damnation and salvation. As Marshall correctly reminds us,

"Progressive environmentalists usually recoil at the accusations of faith, protesting that they are 'atheists'. They are not. At their least religious they are spiritualists that embrace mysticism and superstition. Others are devout in a variety of nature cults that have not yet coalesced into a coherent faith – but they will…

"Monetary absolution is a theme favoured by the cult of Climate Change. Radicalised teachers, media personalities, 'scientists', and politicians fill the national soul with apocalyptic guilt – laying the blame on hot and heavy until the demoralised public drag their wallets to the ATO [i.e.; Australian Taxation Office] and empty them in prayers. Tax the poor, save the planet.

"Children, in particular, are traumatised into believing they are sinful by birth – that their existence is a carbon burden on the planet and a selfish act by their parents. To atone for being born, they are brainwashed into upholding the faith of global apocalypse and supporting political leaders – as a moral duty – who legislate profitable Net Zero ventures".[2]

It is remarkable to witness the return of the ancient gods by the toxic environmentalist cult. Many environmental activists are Gaia worshipers of "Mother Earth" who believe that the world has a form of widespread cancer, and that such cancer is called the human race. Their view of the "environment" is intrinsically anti-human and backed by doctrines linked to nature-worship, elitism and neo-paganism.[3] Such activists often attack our Christian tradition for emphasizing "the supremacy of a male God", in contrast to "Mother Earth" in which one must "acknowledge the animistic traditions of our ancestors".[4]

The Christian view of the environment is remarkably different from the one advocated by these Gaia worshippers and perhaps best articulated by St Francis of Assisi. Instead of seeing humans as diabolical creatures who are raping "Mother Earth", St Francis called Earth our sister and viewed humans and nature as united creations under God the Father. This view, of course, confers infinitely more dignity to the human race because it communicates that we should care about our planet *and* about human life.[5]

Naturally, a reasonable concern to avoid pollution and manage our natural resources in a responsible manner is a commendable ethical position. We should take care of the Earth but also help humanity, at the same time. However, the "environmentalist" efforts of governments to cut carbon emissions make energy less affordable and accessible, which drives up the cost of consumer products, stifles economic growth, costs jobs, and imposes especially harmful effects on the Earth's poorest people.[6] Surely, allocating monetary resources to help build sewage treatment plants, enhance sanitation, and provide clean water for poor people would have a greater immediate impact on their plight than would the battle over the alleged man-made "global warming".[7]

By contrast, one of the hallmarks of the modern environmentalist movement is its appalling indifference towards human life. To give an example, on 25 April 2021 a British Vogue article with the title, 'Is Having A Baby in 2021 Pure Environmental Vandalism?' ponders whether having children is an "act of environmental vandalism". The author seriously asks whether it is even "possible to live an ecologically responsible life while adding another person to our [sic] overstretched planet":

"There are few questions more troubling when looking at the current climate emergency than that of having a baby. Whether your body throbs to reproduce, you passively believe that it is on the cards for you one day, or you actively seek to remain child-free, the declining health of the planet cannot help but factor in your thinking".[8]

Of course, concerns about population growth are not new. In 1968, ecologist Paul Ehrlich echoed 18th-century economist Thomas Malthus when he predicted worldwide famine due to overpopulation and advocated immediate action to limit population growth. Ehrlich was an entomologist at Stanford University and his book, *The Population Bomb*, became one of the most influential books of the 20th century. This book not only made the debate on population control perfectly acceptable, but it also "gave a jolt to the nascent environmental movement and fueled an anti-population-growth crusade that led to human rights abuses around the world".[9] According to British writer and journalist Melanie Phillips,

"The obsession with population control has long been central to the environmental movement even though – ever since Thomas Malthus started this hare running in the nineteenth century – the dire predictions of catastrophic overpopulation have proved false over and over again".[10]

Ehrlich's ideas are a natural extension of Malthusian thought. Malthus argued that the world's human population would increase faster than the food supply unless checked by restraints such as war, famine or disease. He also thought that "most people should die without reproducing".[11]

"Sometime in the next 15 years, the end will come", Ehrlich told CBS News in a prophetic tone just following the publication of his book more than 50 years ago.[12] Needless to say, such bizarre predictions never came true. In spite of all the worry, access to food and resources actually increased as population rose.[13] And yet, this has not stopped many environmental activists from continuing to make similarly bizarre statements about the future of our planet. Prince Philip, the late Duke of Edinburgh, in 1988 commented: "In the event that I am reincarnated, I would like to return as a deadly virus, in order to contribute something to solve overpopulation".[14] Clearly, he felt so strongly about this that he later would state the following:

"I just wonder what it would be like to be reincarnated in an animal whose species had been so reduced in numbers that it was in danger of extinction. What would be its feelings toward the human species whose population explosion had denied it somewhere to exist ... I must confess that I am tempted to ask for reincarnation as a particularly deadly virus".[15]

Prince Philip's neo-pagan predilections for reincarnation could be dismissed as another example of the notorious eccentricities of the British royal family. King Charles III is reported to talk to plants and to blame Syria's horrific civil war on climate change![16]Unfortunately, Prince Philip was not alone in comparing the human race to an "infectious disease"[17], a "super-malignancy on the face of the planet"[18], and "the AIDS of the earth".[19]

According to Ingrid Newkirk, director of *People for Ethical Treatment of Animals*, "the millions who died in the Nazi holocaust were equivalent to broiler chickens dying in slaughterhouses".[20] Yet while animals deserve our protection, people apparently do not. She also said: "I don't believe that human beings have the right to life ... This 'right to human life' I believe is another perversion".[21]

IT IS hard to imagine anything more terrifying than living in a culture where human life is made so entirely relative to lesser values. We have come to the point that even a new human life is seen as a threat to the environment, where some candidly contend that new babies represent an undesirable source of greenhouse emission and consumer of natural resources. This type of thinking is leading conversations about the western democracies adopting population control measures similar to the Communist China one-child policy. According to British commentator Melanie Phillips,

"*Environmentalism ... is considered fashionably progressive in the West. A proper concern to avoid pollution and steward the earth's resources in a responsible manner is indeed a forward-looking, ethical position. Yet the modern environmental movement has become associated – just as it was in Nazi Germany – with indifference or contempt for humanity. It draws upon the most reactionary and regressive trains of thought since the Enlightenment. Those who express scepticism at its apocalyptic predictions of climate catastrophe are called antiscientific "flat-earthers", yet it is environmentalists who are consumed by irrationality and a determination to stop science in its tracks, as well as disdain for bearers of reason, mankind*".[22]

Instead of seeing humans as precious creatures conceived in the image of God, humans are perceived as aggressors against a pristine nature.[23] Some environmental NGOs even finance abortion and population control measures based on a belief that "an increase in human population must degrade the environment".[24] "That thinking leads many to insist that abortion rights are integral to any environmental agenda," says James Tonkowich, a scholar at the *Institute on Religion & Democracy* in Washington, D.C.[25]

FORGOING children is now being promoted as environmentally friendly while childless women are doing their bit to reduce the carbon footprint. It is disturbing to observe women who describe abortion as something entirely positive and environmentally friendly. The *Daily Mail* reports a woman who terminated her pregnancy in the belief she was saving the planet – "not produce a new life which would only add to the problem". To justify her decision, she commented:

> "Having children is selfish. It's all about maintaining your genetic line at the expense of the planet ... Every person who is born uses more food, more water, more land, more fossil fuels, more trees and produces more rubbish, more pollution, more greenhouse gases, and adds to the problem of over-population".[26]

Tragically, not only are the young generations being fooled not to have children due to the fear of endangering the planet, they are also killing their unborn children in service of climate goals. Another woman told the *Daily Mail* that having a child will "pollute the planet". "Never having a child was the most environmentally friendly thing we could do", she said. This woman and her fiancé told the newspaper: "We do everything we can to reduce our carbon footprint. But all this would be undone if we had a child".[27]

Unfortunately, there are plenty of 'useful idiots' around who are willfully embracing the more extreme fringes of the oligarchs' death wish and what is becoming an environmentalist cult. They tend to believe that the Earth 'will not survive' unless drastic measures are taken, including the reduction of the population. Some even lament that neither war nor famine are capable of reducing the population enough, and prefer the arrival of a deadly virus to prey on the innocent.

It is a disturbing fascination with the idea that death brings ecological salvation.

Even in the center of environmental ideology, we must be careful of language that refers to humans as an 'invasive virus', a 'plague', or even a 'problem' that needs to be resolved. Such a desire will downgrade human life, and eliminate it off the planet altogether. Those who express these ideas betray a sinister desire to bring death and destruction at a large scale. They reveal a sinister compulsion to eliminate billions of human beings in search of some utopian small number of sustainable survivors.

In summary, the inhuman nature of modern environmentalism must be exposed and we certainly feel very strongly about the need to expose the irrational nature of the neo-pagan environmentalist cult.

6

TOTALITARIAN ROOTS OF THE ENVIRONMENTALIST DEATH CULT

THE MODERN ENVIRONMENTALIST MOVEMENT IS often compared to a pantheistic religion. It certainly contains a vision of sin and repentance, damnation and salvation. At the Copenhagen climate change summit in December 2009, then Prince Charles, now King Charles III, warned that the survival of mankind itself was in peril and that a mere seven years remained "before we lose the levers of control" over the climate. [1]

We should always take care of the environment and be responsible, and, at the same time, help the poor. And yet, if the demands of radical environmentalists were met, they would have a profoundly deleterious effect on world standards of living, particularly among the poorer peoples of the world. [2]

For example, efforts to convince the world governments to cut carbon emissions make energy less affordable and accessible, which drives up the costs of consumer products, stifles economic growth, and imposes especially harmful effects on the poorest people. [3] Arguably, allocating monetary resources to help build sewage treatment plants, enhance sanitation, and provide clean water for poor people would have a greater immediate impact on their plight than would the battle over global warming[4]

We are constantly told that the temperature is increasing, the seas are rising, the ice is shrinking and the polar bears are vanishing. Not one of these claims is supported by the evidence; indeed the opposite is the case.[5] However, the belief that carbon dioxide emissions are heating up the Earth's atmosphere by a catastrophic degree has been afforded the status of incontestable faith. Australia has even created a government minister for "climate change", absurdly suggesting that politicians can influence the weather! It should, therefore, come as no surprise that the Australian government has fanatically embraced the idea that global warming is happening, humans are to blame, and that doing something drastic about it is in Australia's best interest.

Global warming theory rests on the belief that rising CO_2 levels drive up the temperature of the atmosphere. Despite this degree of terrifying environmental alarmism, and crippling government spending to curb "carbon emissions", historically, temperature increases have often preceded high CO_2 levels, destroying this theory of cause and effect. The fact is that the world has always warmed and cooled, and the theory of anthropogenic global warming contradicts what we know historically to be the case. Nonetheless, according to James Paterson, a Senator for Victoria since 2016,

"The public shaming and bullying of any scientist who differs from climate change orthodoxy is eerily reminiscent of a latter-day Salem Witch-trial or Spanish Inquisition, with public floggings meted out – metaphorically speaking – for their thought crimes. Indeed, 'dissenters', as they have also been labeled, suffer ritual humiliation at the hands of

their colleagues and the media, with their every motivation questioned and views pilloried".[6]

The Nazis and the Environment

Curiously, elements of modern environmentalism are beginning to bear more resemblance to a certain totalitarian movement of the past. During the interwar period, there was an association between environmentalists and German nationalists, among whom a number became committed Nazis. "Environmentalists and conservationists in Germany welcomed the rise of the Nazi regime with open arms and hoped that it would bring about legal and institutional changes".[7] According to Kaitlin Smith, a Boston-based scholar and naturalist educator,

"Nazi leadership ardently championed renewable energy, and institutionalized organic farming and land use planning on a level unmatched by any nation past or present. These environmental policies might seem like a welcome departure from the rest of Nazi propaganda, but their environmentalism was actually grounded in the same racist worldview that shaped the Holocaust".[8]

Historians generally agree that Alfred Seifert (1890-1972) "spoke the language of the emerging ecological movement".[9] He has been characterized as "the most prominent environmentalist in the Third Reich." [10] From 1934 onward Seifert headed a group of Nazi officials whose role was to oversee the ecological impact of public works projects sponsored by the Nazi regime. His position became official in 1935 and he continued to oversee projects in the war years, emphasizing that "previous generations had disrupted the 'balance' of the natural world and failed to take a 'holistic view' of the environment".[11] Following this destructive approach, which was "alien to nature", Seifert believed it "had been overcome thanks to the leadership of the Third Reich".[12]

In October 1934, Seifert was portrayed as the paragon of the "truly National Socialist" approach to environmentalism. He, in turn, published a vast number of articles "outlining his amalgam of environmentalism and National Socialism".[13] After repeated requests from fellow Nazi environmentalists, Seifert eventually was promoted to the civilian equivalent of army general in 1944.[14] He was a frequent visitor to the Dachau concentration camp, and "cooperated closely with its head gardener, SS officer Franz Lippert, who was responsible for maintaining biodynamic standards".[15] His collaboration on the Dachau project continued until shortly before the liberation of the camp in 1945."[16]

Above all, most Nazi leaders embraced a pantheistic worldview. Animal welfare was a significant issue for their totalitarian regime. Hermann Göring, one of the most powerful figures in the Nazi dictatorship, was a professed animal lover who, on instructions of Hitler, committed to concentration camps those who violated Nazi animal welfare laws.[17] Heinrich Himmler, the Reichsführer of the Schutzstaffel (SS), was a passionate vegetarian and certified animal rights activist who aggressively promoted the idea of "natural healing".[18] Indeed, "SS training included respect for animal life of near Buddhist proportions".[19]

The Nazis did not show the same level of respect, of course, for the human race. In hindsight, it may not be difficult to reconcile Nazi views with an environment orientation. In the eyes of Nazi environmentalists, "the privations of war encouraged a renewed emphasis on self-sufficiency and sustainability, allowing Germans to find their way back to the soil and its living forces".[20] "For some green-leaning Nazis, the war and destruction were necessary evils since they would bring about a new order that would finally allow the establishment of a better and greener Germany".[21]

Hitler himself was a committed vegetarian who wanted to turn the entire nation vegetarian.[22] In his diaries, Nazi propaganda minister Joseph Goebbels reports private conversations with Hitler, including a December 19, 1939, talk in which Hitler argues that humans "are not removed from other animals".[23] After trying to convince Goebbels on the virtues of vegetarianism, the Nazi leader contended that the human species had evolved from reptiles through mammals, and that he did "not think much of Homo sapiens".[24] Peter Staudenmaier, a history professor at Marquette University, comments:

> "Hitler and Himmler were both strict vegetarians and animal lovers, attracted to nature mysticism and homeopathic cures, and staunchly opposed to vivisection and cruelty to animals. Himmler even established experimental organic farms to grow herbs for SS medicinal purposes. And Hitler, at times, could sound like a veritable Green utopian, discussing authoritatively and in details various renewable sources (including environmentally appropriate hydropower and producing natural gas from sludge) as alternatives to coal, and declaring "water, winds and tides" the energy path of the future".[25]

In his youth, Hitler studied yoga, astrology and various forms of Eastern occultism. The Nazi leader believed that, in the long run, Nazism and Christianity would "no longer be able to exist together".[26] For him, once the Nazis finally prevailed in the war, Germany would be able to restore "their paganism of antiquity" and the Germans embrace a new form of "Mother-Earth" worship as a substitute for the "Jewish bondage of law".[27] According to Nazi philosopher Ernst Bergmann of Leipzig University, the Germans needed to embrace a new spirituality whereby everyone should live in complete harmony with nature. Influenced by "forces of nature", Bergmann stated, the Germans would be "re-born in the womb of Mother Earth" and rediscover "the God that is in us".[28]

Arguably, the idea of cooperation with the natural world appears to be incompatible with the genocidal policies of the Nazi dictatorship. "How could people who espoused a new appreciation for the environment', 'ecological balance' and 'the harmony with nature' have anything to do with Hitler's war of conquest, racial resettlement, and concentration camps?", asks Staudenmaier rhetorically. According to him,

"The seemingly uncanny convergence between blood and soil ideology and modern ecological concepts makes more historical sense when seen in the context of early environmental talk. In the first decades of the twentieth century, in Germany as elsewhere, racial beliefs and environmental sentiments often went hand in hand. A stance that combined landscape aesthetics, ecological concern, and racial pride was not an anomaly, but shared by most conservationists".[29]

After the war, the Nazi leading environmentalist, Seifert, became "a key figure in the postwar environmental movement in Germany".[30] Arguably, the legacy of Nazi environmentalism poses a dilemma for modern environmentalists.[31] If modern environmentalism was to take off, it had to shed its unhappy links with fascism and racial extermination. However, the slogan often advanced by many contemporary environmentalists, "We are neither right nor left but up front", is historically naïve and politically misleading. As Professor Staudenmaier points out,

"The necessary project of creating emancipatory ecological politics demands an acute awareness and understanding of the legacy of classical ecofascism and its conceptual continuities with present-day environmental discourse ... The record of fascist ecology shows that under the right conditions such an orientation can quickly lead to barbarism".[32]

Some of the Nazis' essentially irrationalist anti-humanism remains intrinsic to environmentalist thinking. Accordingly, modern environmentalism generally demonstrates the same disregard for human life. Paul Watson, the founder of the *Sea Shepherd Conservation Foundation*, compares humans to a virus on the planet. He believes that humans are the "AIDS of the earth":

"Humans are presently acting upon this body [the earth's ecosystem] in the same manner as an invasive virus with the result that we are eroding the ecological immune system.

"A virus kills its host and that is exactly what we are doing with our planet's life support system. We are killing our host the planet Earth.

"I was once severely criticized for describing human beings as being the "AIDS of the Earth". I make no apologies for that statement. Our viral like behaviour can be terminal both to the present biosphere and ourselves".[33]

Granted, he expressed an extreme position. Nonetheless, a growing number of environmentalists have equally succumbed to the highly dangerous notion that there is nothing particularly special about human life.

It is hard to imagine anything more terrifying than living in a culture where human life is made relative to lesser values. Instead of seeing humans as precious creatures conceived in the image of God, many environmentalists see humans as a problem and the cause of all the Earth's predicaments, particularly global warming. In their pantheistic worldview, wrote the late Charles Colson,

> *"it is only logical to place the goal of population control above the dignity of human life and to resort to any means available to reduce the human population in order to preserve Mother Nature from being depleted and despoiled. From this perspective, humans are seen as aggressors against a pristine nature".*[34]

James Tonkowich, a scholar at the *Institute on Religion & Democracy* in Washington, D.C., points out that there is a long history of environmentalist thinking that sees humans primarily as consumers and polluters. "That thinking leads many to insist that abortion rights are integral to any environmental agenda," he says.[35]

In this sense, in the December 2007 edition of *Medical Journal of Australia*, Professor Barry Walters contends that "every newborn baby in Australia represents a potent source of greenhouse gas emissions for an average 80 years, not simply by breathing but by the profligate consumption of resources typical of our society".[36]Walters, who describes childbearing as a "greenhouse unfriendly behavior", "wants the Australian government to consider population control measures like China's, with its one-child-per-family policy backed by draconian penalties, sterilization and forced abortions".[37]

The point is that evil can be, and often is, perpetrated under the guise of doing good. The fanatical environmentalists err morally by believing that their vision of "saving the planet" should be imposed regardless of any human cost. Unfortunately, contemporary environmentalist ideas that were central to Nazism – including the ideas about the organic harmony of the earth, the elevation of animal rights and the denigration of humans as enemies of nature – are today vividly presented as the pinnacle of modern environmentalist thinking. Accordingly, it is perfectly reasonable to conclude that modern environmentalism's fundamental opposition to progress and personal freedom propels it straight into the arms of neo-fascism.[38]

7
THE DIMMING OF THE SUN
AN APOCALYPTIC CATASTROPHE

TWO YEARS AGO A DOCUMENTARY, "THE DIMMING: Exposing The Global Climate Engineering Cover-Up"[1], was released by Dane Wigington of GeoEngineering Watch[2]. Now that we have experienced all the obfuscation and cover-ups of the COVID-19 era it is no big stretch of the imagination to believe him. If you haven't seen that documentary we recommend you watch it. The documentary makes the claim that climate engineering has been going on for decades and there has been a massive cover up.

Yahoo Finance reported in August 2019 that "Bill Gates backs plan to tackle climate change by blocking out the sun":[3]

"It sounds like a wacky idea out of science-fiction - but it's funded in part by billionaire Microsoft founder Bill Gates and backed by top scientists at Harvard University.

*The researchers believe that a fleet of specially-designed aircraft could spray sulfate particles into the lower stratosphere **to cool down our planet and offset the effects of climate change**.* (emphasis added)

A test of the technology has been proposed for this year, the Daily Mail reports, with the Stratospheric Controlled Perturbation Experiment (SCoPEx) seeing a bag of carbonate dust released into the atmosphere 12 miles up."

The project was opposed by sensible Swedish environmentalists. As reported on 2 October 2021,

*"... in their letter that the inaugural SCOPEX balloon flight could be the first step toward the adoption of a potentially "**dangerous, unpredictable and unmanageable**" technology."* [4] *(emphasis added)*

Note that the UK already had a feasibility study project of its own about a decade before this.

*"Stratospheric Particle Injection for Climate Engineering (SPICE) was a United Kingdom government-funded climate engineering (geoengineering) research project that aimed to assess the feasibility of injecting particles into the stratosphere from a tethered balloon for the purposes of **solar radiation management**."* [5]

On 2 July 2023, the London newspaper *Daily Mail,* in an article entitled "More gloomy news from Biden! White House says it's open to plan that would BLOCK sunlight from hitting surface of the Earth in bid to limit global warming", reported:[6]

*"The White House has opened the door to **an audacious plan to block sunlight** from hitting the surface of the Earth in a bid to **halt global warming**.*

*Despite some **scientists warning the effort could have untold side effects from altering the chemical makeup of the atmosphere**, President Joe Biden's administration have admitted they're open to the idea, which has **never been attempted before**."* *(emphases added)*

What could go wrong with that? Besides, it is a solution looking for a problem.

Climate changes! It is driven by the Sun, not human activity. And even if you believed humans, with their cattle grazing and farming practices make a contribution, it is infinitesimal compared to the effects of the sun on climate. According to Dr. David Archibald, a Perth-based climate scientist, the impact of carbon dioxide emissions on world temperatures is minuscule, and what has caused the slight warming of the temperature in the last decade of the 20th century was the Sun. In the previous century, the Sun was more active than at any other time since the 'Medieval Warm Period'. As noted by Dr. Archibald,

> "The existence of the Medieval Warm Period is corroborated by the Greenland borehole temperature data, which shows that Greenland was 1.5° C warmer 1,000 ago than it is today ... The regular voyages of the Vikings between Iceland and Greenland were rarely hindered by ice, and many burial places of the Vikings in Greenland still lie in the permafrost".[7]

The peak of the 'Medieval Warm Period' was at least 2° C warmer than today, and the warming over the 20th century is only 0.7° warmer by comparison to the 'Little Ice Age', *a period of wide-spread cooling from around 1300 AD to around 1850 AD* when average global temperatures dropped by as much as 2°C. We have just recovered from that period but, according to Dr. Archibald, what is happening now is the start of another solar cycle that may result in a dramatic drop of average global temperatures.[8]

Consider the Jakobshavn glacier, which is a large outlet glacier in West Greenland. It is "arguably the most important glacier because it discharges the most ice in the northern hemisphere". Eight years ago, it had retreated 2.9 kilometers and was losing 70 meters annually. But for the last few years it has been growing at the same rate, which means it is already back to its original size.[9]

In other words, the Earth is getting cooler and this cooling will accelerate. The role of the Sun in changing climate is therefore a very strong prediction of continuing cooling. The UN/IPCC should be looking at sunspots. There is a strong correlation with the cycles of sunspot number and total solar irradiance, as well as the Sun's internal activity, like coronal mass ejections, which definitely affect global weather.

No wonder the environmentalist movement had to change the name from "global warming" to "climate change". Global warming is subject to empirical refutation with accumulated evidence of cooling. So, when the temperature rises, we hear, "Wow, that's clear evidence of climate change". But when the climate takes a rapid cooling turn, we hear, "Wow, that's more proof of climate change". This is obviously a tautology – anything that happens, no matter what it is, can be attributed to a single theory.

Environmentalism is quintessentially a totalitarian theory. According to Jonah Goldberg, the founding editor of National Review Online and a former editor at National Review, "the beauty about global warming is that it touches everything we do – what we eat, what we wear, where we go. Our 'carbon footprint' is the measure of man".[10]

In other words, the idea of "climate change" is essentially irrefutable, because somewhere, in some way, the climate is always changing.[11] And any theory that is not refutable is not scientific; it is religion.

Nothing could be more all-encompassing and totalitarian than this religious faith in "global warming". Franklin Delano Roosevelt, who served as U.S. President from March 1933 to

April 1945, once contended that human beings in an age of scarcity will find themselves pressed by something he called "necessity".[12] Life requires the satisfaction of necessities like food, clothes and shelter. Hence, Roosevelt insisted that "necessitous men are not free men" and that the State should be able to make people "free from fear".

Of course, the global oligarchy may attempt to fabricate a "climate crisis" so as to sell their own solution, namely big government. So, the government, previously viewed as "a necessary evil" and potential inimical to rights, now becomes the ultimate "savior" and provider of "rights" from cradle to grave. Call this a form of idolatry, if you wish.

To keep global warming to no more than 1.5°C – as called for in the Paris Agreement – the UN states that carbon emissions should be reduced by 45% by 2030 and reach net zero by 2050. As a consequence, the Australian Government has committed itself to achieve net zero emissions by 2050 and to reduce these emissions by 43 per cent below 2005 levels in the next seven years. Likewise, each Australian state has also set interim emissions reduction targets by 2030. For example, Western Australia has committed itself to reduce greenhouse gas emissions by 80 per cent below 2020 levels.[13]

The fact is that carbon dioxide appears to have a minuscule warming effect on the atmosphere, although an increased atmospheric carbon dioxide could have a very positive effect of agricultural productivity.[14] Professor David Bellamy OBE, "the most eminent botanist and conservationist in the United Kingdom", explains that, "far from being a pollutant, carbon dioxide is the most important airborne fertilizer in the world".[15]

Ironically, in a peer-reviewed paper published in 2021,[16] three scientists taught a machine-learning algorithm how to recognize underlying patterns and cycles in the past 320-year sunspot record. The algorithm then predicted the sunspots from 2021 to 2100. It suggested that the current low solar activity is likely to continue until 2050.[17]

Previous solar minima/mini ice ages have brought in wars, social upheaval and regime changes.[18] Many have died in these changes. But also freezing temperatures reduce crop yields and millions die from starvation and cold. However, the global oligarchs believe, or they claim to believe, that "anthropogenic global warming" is real and that carbon emissions are causing this phenomenon. They also believe that they can fix the problem by modifying the Earth's weather. They have been trying this for a long time – in fact, for the last 75 years according to Dane Wigington. It is absolutely a lie to say it has never been attempted before.

Atmospheric and climate manipulation was once considered a "conspiracy theory" along with "chemtrails".[19] We personally did not believe that chemtrails could be real for a long time. That was because we could not understand why some shadow government or deep state oligarchs could willfully risk poisoning the planet which they themselves must also live on.

The consequences could be devastating if you change the soils by spraying the upper atmosphere with heavy metals like aluminum, barium, manganese, strontium, mercury and more. But now, we understand that they are "all in" on global depopulation and are risking everything in their demented goal to "save the planet" for themselves.

Wigington reports that they also spray with micron-sized graphene particles and polymer fibers, which can be used to carry biological agents into the environment. Can you imagine how devastating that could be if they release pathogens to both humans and other life? It could cause a catastrophic depopulation of the planet.

So, the purpose of dimming the sun is to control alleged

"anthropogenic global warming". But at what cost? Massive tree deaths through poisoning of the soils and raging wildfires. Also, massive hailstones resulting from chemical seeding.

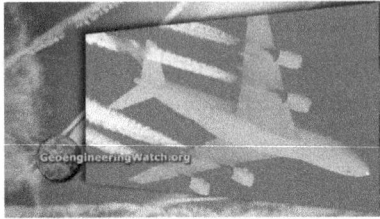

Already geoengineering (chemtrails) has led to the destruction of crops,[20] but globalist media blame it on "global warming". Wigington says it results from the chemical seeding of clouds causing hail formation, which under normal circumstances, would not occur naturally.

Raging wildfires are now becoming a normal occurrence. They also blame this on "global warming". These are now seen across forests in Canada, California and Australia. *Politico* reported on July 6, 2023 with the headline, "'Literally off the charts': Canada's fire season sets records — and is far from over":

*"Officials say the risk will remain high through summer thanks to drought **and above-normal temperatures.**"*

*"'It's no understatement to say that the 2023 fire season is — and will continue to be — **record-breaking**,' Michael Norton, director of the Northern Forestry Centre with the Canadian Forest Service..."*[21]

The chemicals spread across the globe from the deliberate chemtrails are falling to the ground and killing trees everywhere. Consequently, forests are becoming drier and drier. The reduced moisture content in the ground, and poisoned, dried trees resulting in forests burning with a greater intensity. This is not due to "global warming" but poisoning by the maniacs who think they are God with their crazy plan to cool the planet.

Deliberate engineering of floods[22] and droughts on a grand scale has been occurring.[23] The Western half of the USA is in a massive drought.[24] Were they engineered by the dumping of millions of tons of particulate matter into the atmosphere in an effort to dim the sun?

Interestingly enough, all these features were predicted nearly 2,000 years ago in the Book of Revelation. In the last apocalyptic book of the Bible, at the sound of the first trumpet, we read:

> *"The first angel sounded, and there followed **hail and fire mingled with blood, and they were cast upon the earth: and the third part of trees was burnt up, and all green grass was burnt up".** (emphases added) Revelation 8:7*

The prophecy predicts "hail and fire mixed with blood". Droughts can lead to massive fires, and also hailstones, as we have seen, are massive and can cause widespread crop damage. These effects could lead to famine and starvation which could be signified by the expression "mixed with blood". This is also an allusion back to one of the plagues God sent on the Egyptians, which was judgment on the wicked (Exodus 9:22–25).

So let us ask you these questions: Are these effects the result of geoengineering the climate? Could biblical prophecy be fulfilled and the latter be the mechanism God is using in His judgment on the ungodly nations who have rejected Him? We would not be surprised.

Could these maniacal projects of spewing chemical agents into the earth's atmosphere — including heavy metals like aluminum, barium, strontium and others — reflect sunlight and cause a dimming of the sun's energy reaching the surface of the planet? That could cause something like a "nuclear winter". Massive amounts of dust suspended in the upper atmosphere dim the sun alright, but also cause a perpetual winter, where crops fail to grow and millions or billions starve to death.

Bill Gates might accomplish his malicious desire and create global dimming on a massive scale. Is this what was prophesied in Revelation chapter 8 verse 12?

> *"And the fourth angel sounded, and the third part of the sun was smitten, and the third part of the moon, and the third part of the stars; so as **the third part of them was darkened, and the day shone not for a third part of it,** and **the night likewise.**" (emphasis added) Revelation 8:12*

The fact that the scripture says the day and night skies are both dimmed by one third implies extensive atmospheric coverage and that it is persistent. "Blocking the Sun" is the goal. Interfering with the solar energy reaching the Earth's surface will, and probably already has, led to massive crop losses, and global starvation. Who knows what the ingestion of the particulate heavy metals leads to – dementia, Alzheimer's disease and much more?

> *"And the second angel sounded, and as it were a great mountain burning with fire was cast into the sea: and the third part of the sea became blood; 9 And the **third part of the creatures which were in the sea, and had life, died;** and the third part of the ships were destroyed". (emphasis added) Revelation 8:8,9*

Phytoplankton and algae are the major source of oxygen produced on the planet. But phytoplankton populations have been rapidly declining over the past century and have declined by about 70% in the past 70 years.[25] Without phytoplankton – the food source at the bottom of the oceanic food chain – the oceans die.

Could the "mountain burning with fire" (Revelation 8:8) represent the hundreds of millions of tons of particulates (alumina, barium oxide, iron oxides etc) which have not only been killing the oceans, along with all the glyphosate run-off via the rivers and streams, but also the trees and grasses?

> "And the third angel sounded, and there fell a great star from heaven, burning as it were a lamp, and it fell upon the third part of the rivers, and upon the fountains of waters; 11 And the name of the star is called Wormwood: and the **third part of the waters became wormwood; and many men died of the waters, because they were made bitter [poisoned]**." (emphasis added) Revelation 8:10,11

Wormwood is a bitter plant that has a component (Artemisia absinthium) that kills parasites like intestinal worms. Whether or not these verses are symbolic or literal, the judgment includes killing off the parasites on this planet.

"The Dimming" documentary explains the mechanisms behind their maniacal actions. However, Scripture teaches us that God often uses the wicked to judge people for their sins. What the wicked have devised to depopulate the planet with – including bioweapons they call vaccines, engineered famine, engineered diseases, and engineered wars – like with Pharaoh of Egypt, we strongly believe that God will turn back on them in judgment. "So when all these things begin to happen, stand and look up, for your salvation is near!" (Luke 21:28 NLT)

8

EMERGENCY POWERS AND CLIMATE LOCKDOWNS
THE FINAL STEP TO GLOBAL TYRANNY

NOW THAT WE HAVE ENDURED THE TYRANNY OF THE COVID-19 "pandemic" can we relax? No way! The same tyrants are still there and they are planning a lot worse for us than they pulled off during the last scam.

*"The deadliest virus right now is the one that is essential for socialism/**communism** to take hold, and it's spreading rapidly: the crushing of dissent."*[1] (emphases added)

Around the world, especially in so-called "western democracies", laws are being introduced, or already have been passed by legislatures, to ban what they call *misinformation* and *disinformation*. For example, in 2022 the Biden administration in the United States established a 'Ministry of Truth' (an allusion to Orwell's book *1984*):

> *"The Department of Homeland Security has announced the formation of the Disinformation Governance Board—charged, according to Politico, with "countering **misinformation** related to homeland security, focused specifically on irregular migration and Russia."*[2]

That in itself is a cruel joke with the millions crossing the US/Mexico border assisted by the US Department of Homeland Security. But most critically, it turned out that the notorious Nina Jankowicz was chosen to head up the US 'Ministry of Truth' because she is an expert in spreading disinformation. So who else better to spread misinformation?[3]

Recently, the Canadian government has banned media outlets reporting news that they do not approve, Rebel News for example.[4] Likewise, the Australian federal government has just introduced a law proposal in Parliament to ban unapproved online content that they don't agree with.[5,6] The UK also has similar legislation in the works.[7]

There is presently an important discussion to amend the International Health Regulations (2005) (IHR). This would give the World Health Organization (WHO) 'legislative health emergency powers' to undermine every single human right, including the right to access to safe and effective medical products, and the right to not be subject without free consent to medical or scientific forms of experiment. According to Dr. Silvia Behrendt, who holds a PhD on International Health Regulations from Georgetown University, and Professor Amrei Müller, who teaches international humanitarian law at University College Dublin,

"The outcomes of these processes have the potential to affect the livelihoods, lives, health and human rights of individuals around the world, inter alia, because amendments proposed will, if adopted, give unique 'emergency' powers to the WHO and in particular its Director-General (DG), thereby entrenching the securitised approaches to managing infectious disease outbreaks embodied in the so-called Global Health Security (GHS) doctrine that has dominated the WHO-led global response to Covid-19 into international health law".[8]

Australia closely followed the WHO's guidelines since the start of COVID-19 "pandemic". Over this period the Australian Government was 'recommended' by the WHO to implement draconian policies that caused millions of Australians to compromise their health and to endure highly stressful and traumatic situations, including home confinement, job losses and financial ruin. The Australian authorities blindly accepted the entirely alarmist and totally inaccurate WHO's initial prediction of 3.4 per cent mortality for COVID-19 that brought about all these gross violations of fundamental human rights.

One of the measures encouraged by the WHO was the implementation of mandatory vaccination. By the end of 2021 Australia reached a vaccination rate of 80 per cent of the population. Despite having such an impressive vaccination rate, last year (2022) 174,000 deaths were registered in the country, which is 20,000 more than projections estimated. This represents the highest number of excess deaths on record since the end of World War II!

If the changes permitting the WHO and its Director-General to issue legally binding instructions to state members are adopted, these will give the WHO global, legislative, health emergency powers. This is indicated by the proposed policy that changes the currently non-binding temporary "recommendations" on medical and/or non-medical recommendations into *binding* recommendations.

The enactment of these global legislative health policies will transform the WHO's Director-General into a global emergency legislator. This could have disastrous influences with numerous human rights, among them the right to bodily autonomy and the right to safe and effective medical products. Given the WHO's notorious history of collaboration with the pharmaceutical industry, the organization has actively suppressed much important information about the safety of mRNA vaccines as well as the manifold negative effects of lockdowns. According to Dr. Behrendt and Professor Müller,

> *"Under its Emergencies Programme the WHO has established a so-called infodemic unit, through which it enlightens states about what, in its opinion, amounts to health 'mis- or disinformation'... Among other things, it actively tracks social media end-to-end posts in real time in 30 countries and 9 different languages via the Early AI-supported Social Listening platform to rapidly identify spread of alleged misinformation."*[9]

No matter what the news actually is, it is being manipulated and "spun" for the benefit of those who control the levers of power. Global oligarchs, who have for decades complained about overpopulation, appear to have experimented with a deadly bioweapon, called a vaccine, for a disease which was also probably engineered. Emeritus Professor Richard Muller of the Department of Physics at the University of California-Berkeley believes that it is "extremely likely" that the virus was deliberately created in, and released from, the notorious lab at the Wuhan Institute of Virology. Of course, the persuasive theory that COVID-19 virus has not just "escaped" from that CCP virus lab is entirely plausible.

Be that as it may, such a "pandemic" was primarily a test regarding the compliance of the global population. Unfortunately, the global oligarchs have discovered that fear of some invisible virus was very effective in gaining control over the masses. The form of that compliance was seen in the crazy, often contradictory, diktats from governments. Taking an experimental drug, social distancing at 1.5 m (or 6 ft) separation, even outdoors, and mask wearing (even when so-called experts flip-flopped on efficacy) were enforced with fines and, in some cases, jail. But worst of all was the first time ever used practice of lockdowns, outside of a prison.

What is coming next? The so-called environmentalists have claimed that COVID-19 lockdowns were the most successful mitigation action against global warming yet.

Climate lockdowns are now being called for. As stated in an article published by *Technocracy News & Trends*,

> "*If and when the powers-that-be decide to move on from their pandemic narrative, lockdowns won't be going anywhere. Instead it looks like they'll be rebranded as "climate lockdowns", and either enforced or simply held threateningly over the public's head.*"[10]

According to 'Avoiding a climate lockdown', an article written by an employee of the WHO, and which has been published by both a Gates/Soros backed NGO and a group representing almost every bank, oil company and tech giant on the planet,

> "*Under a "climate lockdown," governments would limit private-vehicle use, ban consumption of red meat, and impose extreme energy-saving measures, while fossil-fuel companies would have to stop drilling. To avoid such a scenario, we must **overhaul our economic structures and do capitalism differently.**"*[11] (emphasis added)

There it is. It is not about reducing global temperatures. It is about communism with Chinese (CCP) characteristics. In fact, all the discussion on global temperature, which we hear incessantly now, is a distraction from the real agenda revealed here.

In the northern hemisphere they are saying that this summer is unlike anything we have ever seen before. Many are saying the summer of 2023 feels like the planet has been thrown into an extremely hot oven. Temperatures are record-breaking![12] July 4th, 2023 was claimed to be the hottest day in 125,000 years.[13]

But there is no mystery. The Sun is more active in this solar cycle (number 25) now than in the previous cycle (number 24). The number of sunspots currently being observed exceeds anything that we have witnessed during the last solar cycle.[14] It looks like they will peak earlier than the modeling predicted. So in this current solar cycle, more sunspots means more activity in the Sun and hence hotter temperatures on Earth.

However, the overall reduction of sunspots over the past several 11-year sunspot cycles (see cycles 22 through 25 in Fig.1) means the solar radiation is reducing (Fig. 2) and thus the planet is headed into a much cooler period, even a mini ice age.[15,16]

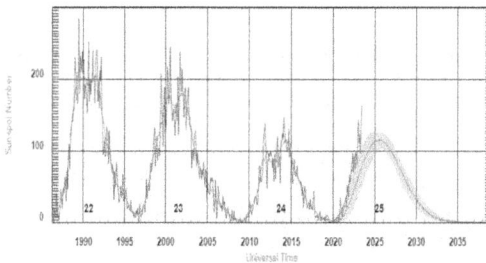

Figure 1: Sunspot number as a function of time taken from NOAA data. The numbers 22 to 25 indicate the approx. 11 year solar cycles.[17] Red curve is the modeled average number of sunspots hence in cycle 25 it is the expected number from the model. The gray curve is the measured sunspot number.

As indicated by the plot in Fig. 1 the sunspot number is above that expected and this means the sun is more active than the model predicted.[18] The modeling here got it wrong and this science is well developed with almost 400 years of sunspot data.

Can you imagine how wrong the global warming models can be with only 4 decades of satellite temperature data? The rest are highly debatable tree ring proxies that Michael Mann relied upon in the now infamous "hockey-stick" plot. But that isn't all. It was found that the "hockey-stick" data were incorrectly manipulated.[19]

"Suddenly the hockey-stick, the poster-child of the global warming community, turns out to be an artefact of poor mathematics."

That means it is now fundamental to the measurements but introduced by the statistical method used. The global-warming climate-change cult must protect the big lie at all costs. The authors of the research that discovered this error were themselves rejected from the world's leading science journal when they tried to publish their paper. As reported:

"McIntyre and McKitrick sent their detailed analysis to Nature magazine for publication, and it was extensively referenced. But their paper was finally rejected. In frustration, McIntyre and McKitrick put the entire record of their submission and the referee reports on a Web page for all to see (go to ref.[20])."

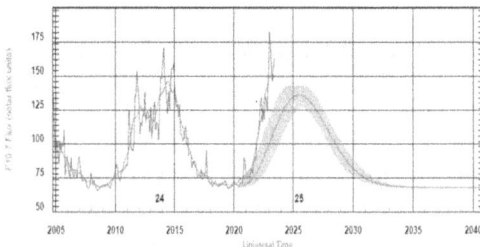

Figure 2: Solar flux (radiation) as a function of time taken from NOAA data. The numbers 24 to 25 indicate the approx. 11 year solar cycles.[21] Red curve is the modeled average solar flux hence in cycle 25 it

is the expected flux from the model. The gray curve is the measured solar flux.

Now let's look at the radiation flux from the Sun. From Fig. 2 solar flux data it is clear that the prediction (red curve) for expected flux is far lower in value than the measured flux. High flux means more radiation from increased solar activity.

Increased activity includes strong solar flares and coronal mass ejections (CMEs), large clouds of ionized plasma that are ejected from the Sun's outer atmosphere. These solar storms generated by the Sun can have a damaging effect on electric power grids, GPS and communication satellites and aviation. Also we expect to see more seismic activity, volcanism and earthquakes.

Many large earthquakes have struck in 2023.[22] On July 16th 2023, a 7.2-magnitude earthquake struck off the southern Alaskan coast,[23] July 18th, a 6.5-magnitude earthquake struck off El Salvador's Pacific coast.[24]

Now it needs to be understood, increased solar activity usually means higher temperatures.[25] But this is evidence against man-made global warming. If the solar activity is causing the Earth changes, and space weather events, then it is not from human activity.

However, we do not deny that the Earth is warming and it has gone through warming periods in the past. See Fig. 3. It is, but not like the myriads of models indicate. Many of the predictions of the climate cult have never materialized.

Use of tree rings as a proxy for past temperatures is flawed science. In 2008, Craig Loehle and J. Huston McCulloch published a paper[26],[27] that described why tree rings cannot be trusted[28] as a proxy for past temperature variations. Tree-ring data have what is called a "divergence problem" in the late 20th Century where the tree ring data suggested cooling, when in fact there had been warming. This, by itself, should cast serious doubt on whether tree-ring reconstructions (such as Michael Mann's famous "hockey stick" curve) can be used to estimate past global temperature variability.

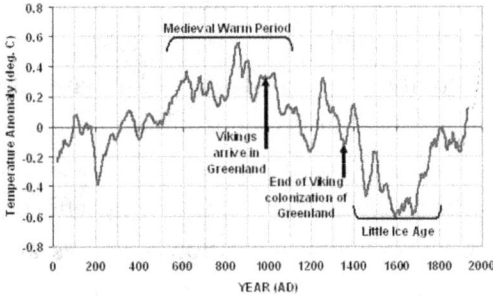

Figure 3: This graph shows the average of 18 non-tree ring proxies of temperature from 12 locations around the Northern Hemisphere, published by Craig Loehle in 2007, and later revised in 2008. It clearly shows that natural climate variability happens, and these proxies coincide with known events in human history.[29]

We were told that hydrological processes were expected to intensify with warming. That is processes like storms, hurricanes and precipitation would become much worse. But a new study, published May 2023, shows that precipitation in this century compared to last century has become less intense globally.[30] The opposite trends from 2001 to 2020 were measured compared to that expected.

"Small and medium size "precipitation systems" have reduced in intensity in summer and winter and all over the globe. More widespread systems are a wash with some up and some down, and none of it in a pattern that climate models predicted."[31]

So let's not get distracted. There is no "climate emergency"!

The **World Climate Declaration**[32] has been signed by at least 1500 scientists of the Global Climate Intelligence Group (www.clintel.org). You can find a full list of the signatories here.[33]

One of the authors of this book (Prof. John G. Hartnett) has also signed it. The Declaration states:

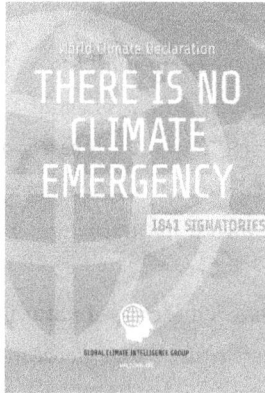

"A global network of over 1501 scientists and professionals has prepared this urgent message.

Climate science should be less political, while climate policies should be more scientific. Scientists should openly address uncertainties and exaggerations in their predictions of global warming, while politicians should dispassionately count the real costs as well as the imagined benefits of their policy measures.

Natural as well as anthropogenic factors cause warming

The geological archive reveals that Earth's climate has varied as long as the planet has existed, with natural cold and warm phases. The Little Ice Age ended as recently as 1850. Therefore, it is no surprise that we now are experiencing a period of warming.

Warming is far slower than predicted

The world has warmed significantly less than predicted by IPCC on the basis of modeled anthropogenic forcing. The gap between the real world and the modeled world tells us that we are far from understanding climate change.

Climate policy relies on inadequate models

Climate models have many shortcomings and are not remotely plausible as global policy tools. They blow up the effect of greenhouse gasses such as CO_2. In addition, they ignore the fact that enriching the atmosphere with CO_2 is beneficial.

CO_2 is plant food, the basis of all life on Earth

CO_2 is not a pollutant. It is essential to all life on Earth. Photosynthesis is a blessing. More CO_2 is beneficial for nature, greening the Earth: additional CO_2 in the air has promoted growth in global plant biomass. It is also good for agriculture, increasing the yields of crops worldwide.

Global warming has not increased natural disasters

There is no statistical evidence that global warming is intensifying hurricanes, floods, droughts and suchlike natural disasters, or making them more frequent. However, there is ample evidence that CO_2-mitigation measures are as damaging as they are costly.

Climate policy must respect scientific and economic realities

There is no climate emergency. Therefore, there is no cause for panic and alarm. We strongly oppose the harmful and unrealistic net-zero CO_2 policy proposed for 2050. If better approaches emerge, and they certainly will, we have ample time to reflect and re-adapt. The aim of global policy should be 'prosperity for all' by providing reliable and affordable energy at all times. In a prosperous society men and women are well educated, birthrates are low and people care about their environment.

The World Climate Declaration (WCD) has brought a large variety of competent scientists together from all over the world. The considerable knowledge and experience of this group is indispensable in reaching a balanced, dispassionate and competent view of climate change.

From now onward the group is going to function as "Global Climate

Intelligence Group". The CLINTEL Group will give solicited and unsolicited advice on climate change and energy transition to governments and companies worldwide."

In September 2022, the United Nations' General Assembly adopted Resolution 75/1, which contains a declaration emphasizing "the need to improve ... preparedness for not only health-related crises but also other challenges and crises".[34]

In September 2024, the United Nations (UN) will host 'The Summit of the Future', where member states will be invited to adopt an agreement to consolidate globalist policy reforms offered over the past two years, including the U.N. 2030 Agenda and the Paris Climate Agreement.

'Our Common Agenda' is described as the ultimate vision of the United Nations for "strengthening global governance for present and future generations".[35] This comprehensive document contains even a plan for "emergency platforms" to respond to "complex global shocks".[36] The "global response" to COVID-19, one finds in the document, was "insufficient" because of the lack of "global mechanisms" to ensure that all countries have "access to vaccines".[37]

Further details of the "emergency platform" are laid down in a March 2023 policy paper entitled 'Strengthening the International Response to Complex Global Shocks – An Emergency Platform'.[38] The policy paper says that the U.N. secretary-general should have the "authority to convene and operationalize automatically an Emergency Platform in the event of a future complex global shock of sufficient scale, severity and reach". The range of risks that could activate "the emergency platform" is "broad and diverse", although future pandemic risks, "global digital connectivity disruption", and climate change, are cited as examples of "global shocks" that require the activation of the emergency platform.[39]

The policy paper then explains that the emergency platform could be instituted for a finite period to respond to any specific "global shock". However, "at the end of that period the Secretary-General could extend the work of an Emergency Platform if required", according to the U.N.'s own official policy proposal.[40] This basically means that the U.N. secretary-general would have the legislative power to keep an "emergency platform" in place indefinitely. The late Austrian-British economist and philosopher, Friedrich Hayek, a Nobel Prize laureate, once offered this sobering reflection about the continuing renewal of emergency powers by tyrannical regimes:

> "*The conditions under which emergency powers may be granted without creating the danger that they will be retained when the absolute necessity has passed are among the most difficult and important points a constitution must decide on. 'Emergencies' have always been the pretext on which the safeguards of individual liberty have been eroded – and once they are suspended it is not difficult for anyone who has assumed such emergency powers to see to it that the emergency will persist.*"[41]

We are witnessing here the first steps towards the constitution of global tyranny. Detailed protocols will be developed in order to make sure that the secretary-general is endowed with full legislative mandate "to convene and operationalize an Emergency Platform" that covers "a range of scenarios".[42]

It goes without saying that the U.N. secretary-general, Antonio Guterres, is an active member of the Portuguese Socialist Party. Writing in *The Spectator Australia*, Dr. Graham Pinn, comments that "*Guterres seems more interested in saving the planet from climate change than war; he is also leading the organization in its wealth redistribution agenda, with the Great Reset of capitalism (no mention of communism). The Great Reset is supported by other influential people such as Klaus Schwab of the World Economic Forum, King Charles III, socialists in the US, business leaders, high profile politicians, and activists, with its intention being to reset the world economy after Covid; as this is fading climate change will regain its role as the new world threat."*[43]

The implementation by the U.N. secretary-general of an emergency protocol would have the immediate effect of suspending any basic human right in the face of "complex global shocks", including "climate change".[44] This suspension of human rights could be interpreted as a perfectly valid way to respond to "the type and nature of the crisis involved".

In *Political Theology*, a book published in 1922, the Nazi legal philosopher, Carl Schmitt, contended that the use of emergency powers "exempts the authority from every normative restraint and renders it absolute in the true sense of the word". "In a state of emergency", he concluded, "the constituted authority suspends the law on the basis of the right to protect its own existence".[45]

Of course, the real agenda is the global implementation of a Chinese Communist Party (CCP) style communism, a World Economic Forum (WEF) stakeholder capitalism, where the middle class is eliminated and all their private property confiscated. The middle class will join the working poor in a new serfdom they call the New World Order. The implementation of climate lockdowns is just another step in tyranny to take control of the global economic system by the globalist banksters in what they call the Great Reset courtesy of the WEF.

Those well informed people are not fooled but, as the WEF has infiltrated much of the western governments and controls the mass media, it seems that there is no stopping this advance to totalitarianism. Their next step under the UN Agenda 2030 and WEF Great Reset plan is convincing you to accept their 15-minute cities. The "15-minute city" is by another name a "climate lockdown". They say that they care about you, they want you to drive less. Just to keep you healthy and happy, of course (sarcasm alert). Australia's climate researcher Jo Nova wrote in regards to this:[46]

"In the WEF's own words[47]— this rearrangement of cities is absolutely about climate change:

As climate change and global conflict cause shocks and stresses at faster intervals and increasing severity, the 15-minute city will become even more critical.

And the solution was the pandemic (they really say that):

The obvious, yet incomplete, answer is the pandemic.... with COVID-19 and its variants keeping everyone home (or closer to home than usual), the 15-minute city went from a "nice-to-have" to a rallying cry. Meeting all of one's needs within a walking, biking or transit distance was suddenly a matter of life and death".

The totalitarians want to confine us to their 15-minute gulags. They use all nice sounding language but ultimately it is to confiscate your private property, especially your car, and to herd you into the ghettos. They are working with city councils – Jo Nova discusses the Oxfordshire County Council -- which wants to divide the city of Oxford into six 15-minute districts. Sounds like ghettos to us.

But the fact checkers (USA Today) claimed that the report on Oxfordshire County Council originating at the "Watts Up With That" website is misleading. The fact-checkers stated:[48]

"The article misconstrues the facts around a new traffic reduction plan approved by the Oxford County Council in Oxfordshire, U.K., in

November. The new traffic reduction system will restrict drivers from accessing certain main roads during daytime hours through the use of 'traffic filters'."

This may be true but do not be distracted by the obfuscation of the real underlying plan which the WEF openly discusses. What if this was a small test to see if they could incrementally introduce a 15-minute city without the residents noticing?

We know many city councils are discussing "15-Minute City" plans. According to a recent report:[49]

"Canterbury has published plans to divide the city into 5 "traffic zones." London is planning the expansion of ultra low emission zones ("ULEZ"). Bristol and Sheffield Councils have signed up to the plans to restrict freedom of movement within the cities. Swansea Council has also confirmed plans to become a 15-minute city. Lancaster is attempting to sell their dystopian 15-minute neighborhood plan by comparing it to "becoming like Amsterdam." And Scotland has published plans to implement 20-minute neighborhoods nationwide".

The People's Voice reported"[50]

"The 15 minute city concept, the brainchild of the World Economic Forum in Davos, Switzerland, is becoming a reality in the United States with the city of Cleveland, Ohio signing up to the scheme and vowing to implement Klaus Schwab's vision.

According to the globalists promoting the concept, 15 minute cities are necessary to fight climate change and support public health.

Democrat Mayor Justin Bibb says he is determined to make Cleveland, Ohio the first 15-minute city in North America, introducing the concept to local residents and media during his State of the City speech in April last year.

"We're working toward being the first city in North America to implement a 15-minute city planning framework, where people—not developers, but people—are at the center of urban revitalization, because regardless of where you live, you have access to a good grocery store, vibrant parks, and a job you can get to," Bibb said in the speech."

The plan is to move all the remaining population (after the initial bioweapon and geoengineering culls) into these cities and off the land so that the wild spaces can regrow according to those lunatics at the WEF. The first move of any totalitarian is to move the undesirable class into ghettos. Once you have them there, you can then more easily cull the herd. Don't be deceived by their flattering words like "sustainability, equity and diversity".

As designed by the tyrannical global oligarchy, the power exercised via the emergency platform would be completely devoid of any legal limits. Since this would lead to a form of 'legalized arbitrariness' at global scale, what would follow is the complete elimination of *any* basic human right as these rights could be suspended until further notice as a result of the emergency platform having to tackle issues such as a "climate emergency".

As can be seen, the approval of the emergency platform by the member states of the United Nations, Australia included, would comprise the final step towards the institutionalization of a global dictatorship based on the principles of International Socialism, thus conferring to a few oligarchs the power to exercise absolute control over the lives of every human being on this planet.

In other words, if the emergency platform becomes a reality, the world as we know it will basically cease to exist. We either fight against this tyrannical idea or risk losing everything come September 2024.

9
THE FOUR HORSEMEN HERALD THE MARK OF THE BEAST

Four Horsemen of the Apocalypse, an 1887 painting by Viktor Vasnetsov. Public Domain

CHAPTER 6 OF THE BOOK OF REVELATION OPENS WITH the first horse, a white horse. He is one of four horsemen who bring death on Earth. The other three horsemen are listed as being red for war, black for famine, and pale green for plagues. First let's look at the white horse. What is his significance?

*"And I saw, and behold a **white** horse: and he that sat on him had a* *bow; and a **crown** was given to him: and he went forth conquering, and* *to conquer."* —Revelation 6:2

It is worth noting that the current global COVID-19 "plandemic" has been engineered with the initial release of a bioweapon called SARS-CoV-2 virus and then that was followed up with more deadly bioweapons, which they call "vaccines". We call them *"toxxines"*, because they are *toxic*, and not a true vaccine. The Spike protein in the "vaccines" is pathogenic and infects the whole body, leading eventually to death in most recipients.

These so-called "vaccines" were and are delivered by what is currently called the "health system", which should really be called the "death system". They were developed by medical research scientists (mentioned previously). People in these professions wear white lab coats as some type of uniform. That fits in with the picture of the white horse.

What else can that verse above tell us about the nature of this horseman who was sent by God to wreak havoc and death on Earth? The English word "bow" is translated from the Greek word "toxon" from which the English words "toxin" and "toxoid" are derived.

In a Tetanus shot the patient is given an antitoxin, for example. This is made with a toxoid, which is "a substance that has been treated to destroy its toxic properties but retains the capacity to stimulate production of antitoxins, used in immunization."

Related to "toxon" is the word "toxikon" which means a poison arrow. So probably we should look at the verse as describing the weapons system of a bow and arrows where the arrows are tipped with poison. From this we can see that the real nature of the weapons system the rider of the white horse uses is the COVID-19 toxin, which they falsely call a "vaccine".

The rider wears a crown, which is translated from the Greek word "stephanos" meaning the laurels that a winner or victor receives. This would represent a strong man, not necessarily a king or ruler, but someone with power and strength. He conquers by the power of the toxins he uses to inject mankind.

Interestingly the bioweapon used was built with a coronavirus. The virus particle, called a virion, has a crown of spikes, hence the name *corona*-virus. Perhaps this is symbolized in the crown worn by the rider of the white horse.

The white horse is only one of the four horses of the Apocalypse (see Revelation chapter 6). Since it appears that the first horseman represents an engineered form of death (from the COVID-19 shots) then why wouldn't the other three also represent engineered forms of death, through wars, famine and plagues (like Smallpox, Anthrax, Ebola etc)?

Could it be that we are seeing this play out now? Mass extinction of much of the human race, as prophesied in the Book of Revelation chapters 6, 8 and 9? The extinction is all engineered by evil men but is actually God's judgments on the world because they have forgotten their Creator.

The horsemen do not come in a sequence but all at the same time, yet it does seem that the white horse is the leader. This is the same as we saw in the last 3 years. First the bioweapon was released from a Chinese virology lab, then the world economic system was shut down in a pre-planned coordinated program. Then during the years of lockdowns, mandatory vaccination, economic shutdowns and new totalitarian laws were quietly being enacted along with new surveillance techniques (cameras, digital facial recognition etc) that were put in place.

The more we read the news the more we see the development of a universal, tracking, control system that the Book of Revelation describes as *the mark of the beast*. And this is now being implemented rapidly.

A key Bible verse taken from the book of Revelation chapter 13 verses 16 and 17 states:

*"And he causes all, both small and great, rich and poor, free and bond, to receive a mark in their right hand, or in their foreheads: And that no man might buy or sell, save he that had **the mark**, or the name of the beast, or the number of his name."*

A mark can be a certificate, a pass, or a passport. It is a means of identification.

Australian banks and other businesses are currently building an electronic system with a QR code called eQR that links to EFTPOS payment systems[1] and several large supermarkets have already signed up. These include Woolworths and Coles, the two largest grocery retailers in Australia.

The QR code is currently used to track the location of the herd. To this will be added a digital ID,[2] for which federal legislation was already passed into law in 2019 and added to in 2021. You will soon need to provide 100 points of ID to engage in social media. It will be the end of online anonymity.

Current legislation being worked on will create what they call "Trusted Digital Identity Framework"[3] to manage the digital ID. It also has an added biometric component, which means that your smartphone can scan your fingerprint, voiceprint or facial features to identify you.

In addition, at least 57 countries have already accepted the *Common Pass* electronic Vaccine Passport system, related to *Smart* health card, powered by Microsoft Azure. And with a new rice-grain-size injectable,[4] your temperature and health status can be monitored on the block chain. Add to that Bill Gates patent with number ending in ....060606[5]—a patent for a digital currency created from sensors embedded in your body[6]—and you are well on the way to *the mark of the beast*.

The next step in Australia will be to freeze the Australian Business Numbers (ABNs) and tax file number (TFNs) of the unvaccinated. Without an ABN you cannot run a business and get paid. Without a tax file number (TFN) you cannot get paid for your labor, and that means no job. Without getting the COVID-19 vax, or whatever they introduce next, you cannot get these or an eQR digital identity pass. This is not about your immunity to a disease, it is about you getting the shots, which seem to make people much more compliant.

How insane is this? A bioweapon released was used as an excuse for the rapid development of another bioweapon, which they are calling "vaccines".

No vax, no job and hence no pay! This is extreme coercion. It should never occur; this is a free, democratic society. But this is Marxism/Fascism[7] : rule by the government diktats in cahoots with big corporations. Or as Klaus Schwab calls it–stakeholder capitalism–not free market capitalism, which has been extinguished already.

The eQR code system will very quickly lead to a cashless system. Already, some stores and individual banks are refusing cash. This will also mean that if you are unvaccinated and don't have a valid eQR code then you cannot transact online. Thus, no ability to purchase food online and have it delivered or pick it up at a store, let alone enter a shopping center.

The eQR code/vaccine passport will need to be kept up to date with the latest round of booster shots, and more vaccines for the next plagues they release. Failing to get the next booster in the endless series means you lose your "green" status. That is the same as being unvaccinated. This was successfully demonstrated in China during 2021-2023.

Note, when Pfizer trialed booster shots on animals, they prepared to give the 2 shot COVID-19 toxin injections followed by 6 boosters. But no animal in the trials survived past the 3rd booster. That is only the fifth shot in the series.

Next the Australian government will re-introduce the once shelved "cash ban" legislation that was aimed at eventually eliminating all cash from circulation. It was to start with banning cash transactions greater than $10,000, and eventually eliminate cash all together, leading to a cashless society. The same is happening in most Western nations.

Already some banks are closing off their teller windows to deliver any cash at all. The ANZ bank in Australia is one bank doing this as others are tightening restrictions on the amount of cash a depositor can take in a day. Note that this is the customer's own money. A piece of legislation that passed in 2018 has turned all depositors into unsecured creditors. That means you are loaning the money to the bank and it is no longer yours.

That was Australia's "bail in" law, designed to take the depositors money when the banks go insolvent. We suspect that most of the large retail banks are already insolvent if you include their risky investments in the highly leveraged derivatives market. They are hiding this fact with all the cheap money from central bank currency printing. If they go bust, which looks increasingly likely, the depositors (as unsecured creditors) would be last to get any of their money back. In 2010, when the banks in Cyprus failed, the depositors were given shares in the failed banks, which were worth only about 6 cents in the dollar. Their money was even taken from foreign banks of the EU zone.[8] To add to this, there is massive money printing in the US, with inflation now running at 14% (at the time of writing this book), making the crash of the US dollar imminent.

In 2023 it seems that the global cabal has already put in place a social credit system (ESG) like that in China. For example, like the "Bud Light" beer (Anheuser-Busch) fiasco,[9] the large corporations are already more interested in their ESG score by enforcing wokeness than serving their customers. This type of social credit system could be used to restrict your access to travel, and more importantly, to food. But most of all, it is a control system that ultimately will be used to control all online speech. You will not be able to criticize the actions of the government. That will be called "hate speech" and "domestic terrorism".

The *Australian Surveillance Legislation Amendment (Identify and Disrupt) Act 2021*[10] allows the government to invade your online social media accounts, alter or delete posts, as well as act as you and write whatever they choose, even committing crimes in your name, as if you were the one doing the crime.

If that wasn't enough, Pfizer was reported to be developing a twice-daily pill[11] to be taken by the vaccinated. Pfizer says it will prevent COVID-19 symptoms, but really it is to counteract adverse reactions from the COVID-19 toxin injections. It is even a *red pill* and an antiviral designed to work like Ivermectin, but modified, so they can patent it and make a lot more money.

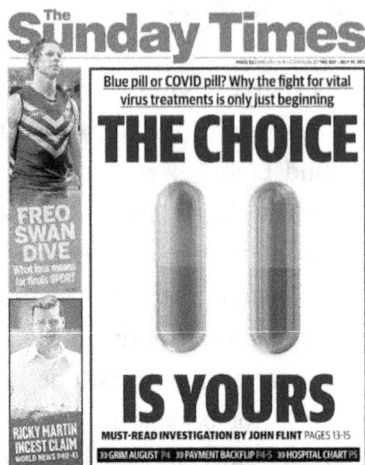

The Sunday Times (Western Australia), July 17, 2022. The headline uses the metaphor from the movie The Matrix, *falsely comparing the COVID pill to the Red Pill of truth and freedom.*

IT WILL BE NEEDED FOREVER by those who take it because, in my opinion, it will be quite addictive and needed to fend off the adverse reactions of endless boosters. Creative psychology will be, and has been, used to drive people to keep taking it. Unless they have been really *red-pilled* somehow, they will live in constant fear of getting the dreaded COVID-19 disease. They become customers for life, however long or short that may be for those who have taken the Spike protein bioweapon shots.

The oligarchs implementing this Marxist takeover are the usual culprits: Big Pharma, Big Banks, Big Tech, GAVI, Gates, Soros, Club of Rome, WEF, Bilderbergers, Rockefellers, Rothschilds, Illuminati, Freemasons and Jesuits, all of which Jesus referred to as the Synagogue of Satan. Some call them the evil Khazarians, but they are the rich and powerful who control most of the major corporations of the world.

FROM REVELATION 18:23 we read

> *... for your merchants were* **the great men of the earth;** *for by your* **sorceries** *were all nations deceived.*

The Greek word translated here as 'sorceries' is pharmakia from which we derive words like pharmacy and pharmaceuticals. Big Pharma are sorcerers.

Now, once addicted to their daily drug through the deception of their sorcery (mainstream media and drugs), you will only be able to buy through the cashless, QR-linked vaccine-passport and tracked, digital ID credit system.[12] So those who take it will be caught in a trap. The boosters will eventually kill them, and they will pay for the twice daily pills until they are dead or until they have lost their minds.

Watch out for the next round! A new plague with an accompanying fear campaign to get people to take the next toxin is coming.

Add to this the engineered food shortages and engineered financial collapse via which the deep state cabal will steal privately owned property and we'll see a full Marxist takeover of the country. We believe that the Australian state and federal governments are following the script of the "Great Reset", which requires weakening food security by eventually taking land from the farmers. The plans to compromise food security and destroy our property rights are well underway in Australia.

Australia tried to alter its Constitution to give an unelected body permanent power to veto any federal legislature, all in the name of "justice" and "equity" for the Indigenous people. The campaign was called the "Voice to Parliament". Activists said it was for a redistribution of power through a treaty; one activist even mentioned communism (done right this time, of course). Voters made an outcry and the bill was defeated, for now.

Similar "de-colonization" anti-white proposals are underway in other Western countries. Using the Indigenous peoples is a common tactic of the Marxists.

Let me ask this question: where is the church in this? Most, but thankfully not all, church leaders have been swayed by government and mainstream media propaganda. Or they have been lulled to sleep by the easy life and easy money. They certainly are not standing against the evils of the Luciferians who are taking over the world and ushering in their New World Order.

Instead many church leaders promoted the COVID-19 toxins, which have had an appalling toll on those which have been deceived into taking them. Franklin Graham recommended the experimental Moderna and Pfizer toxins, saying they have no aborted fetal tissue in them. True, but they use murdered baby cells in the testing phase. The Samaritan's Purse's President said, *"I think if there were vaccines available in the time of Christ, Jesus would have made reference to them and used them."* [13] What utter nonsense! Jesus is the Creator of the universe. He is the greatest Physician of all. He healed the sick everywhere He went. He didn't need vaccines and certainly didn't need bioweapons to kill people. That is how deceiving Lucifer operates.

One of us was told by a practicing witch that they recommend the vaccines and she had taken them all. This shows you the connection between sorcery, the occult and the toxic shots.

Interestingly Franklin Graham, the president and CEO of the Billy Graham Evangelistic Association and of Samaritan's Purse, had heart surgery to fix a problem he recently developed, that is, constrictive pericarditis. [14] He was double jabbed with the COVID-19 shots. Pericarditis, inflammation of the sac around the heart, is a symptom of those shots.

A classic example of the church serving an oppressive system: In November 2021, the Catholic Archbishop of Brisbane, Mark Coleridge, issued a "strongly worded ultimatum" for all priests within his diocese to be fully vaccinated. Coleridge said that "personal choice" was "outweighed" by obligations to COVID-19-related public health directives and a "duty of care" to parishioners. "I will not consider a conscientious objection to receiving the vaccination as a valid exception to the provisions set out here", he added.[15]

Archbishop Coleridge's decision to impose a vaccine mandate on all Catholic priests based on the duty of care was irrational and illogical because the concept of bodily autonomy and the right to life is crucial in Catholic tradition– they are both derived from the traditional principles of natural law. Further, if the "vaccine" really is an effective method of protection, then anybody who takes the jab should not be concerned about infection from the unvaccinated. Of course, this is not the case and, according to Zimmermann, Coleridge should face legal liability from clergy who experienced any "adverse side-effects" from such a "vaccine".[16]

The problem is that the church has joined the world. They have become the establishment instead of being a firebrand, warning the world of man's sin and calling sinners to repentance. The church is afraid to warn the governments of man against their evil actions. The church is lost in idol worship of the world. As the mainstream media cancels any alternative voice warning of the coming *mark of the beast*, where is the voice of the church?

All the anti-science transgenderism and the LGBTQ+ push is against the divine law. This will lead to the inclusion of P for pedophile in this list.[17] The murder of millions of unborn babies is a horrible sin. The Satanists claim the rights to murder babies in the womb in their satanic rituals. [18] The world now openly accepts Satanism which has been decisively now linked to transgenderism and the gay agenda.

This current COVID-19 "vaccination" program is nothing short of eugenics and premeditated mass murder. The church should be calling out the sin, and standing against the tyranny of vaccine mandates and all the life-destroying "health directions" of the state and federal governments.

God is holy and He will not allow sin to flourish. As a result, we believe what we are seeing now is **the work of God**. This is the beginning of a mass extinction event. It is the beginning of God's judgments. And you cannot stop God.

God does not commit acts of evil but He sure uses the actions of evil men to bring about His purposes. What we are seeing now is Jesus' Great Reset. He is calling some of us out of the darkness and the rest are condemning themselves to hell by their own actions.

*And the smoke of their torment ascends up for ever and ever: and they have no rest day nor night, who worship the beast and his image, and whosoever receives the **mark** of his name. —Revelation 14:11*

Evil waxes worse and worse. There is no solution to the globalist takeover while the tsunami is coming. We need to wait until the wave crashes. Then we can start to rebuild. We need to look to Jesus and trust in His power to subdue evil and bring His kingdom down to Earth. This will then be **Christ's New World Order.**

We believe what we'll eventually see is a glorious victory over evil. But we must go through some hard times to get there. Be prepared for the days when God will judge all the wicked ones who engineered the global *pandemic* and are currently mass murdering billions with their COVID-19 toxins, engineered wars, engineered famines, and engineered plagues.

In addition, the oligarchs are pushing the fake global warming agenda when, in fact, the Earth is heading into a little ice age, due to the Sun going into hibernation.[19] This is what we call the Grand Solar Minimum: sunspot numbers reduce, with each solar cycle. However, as we approach solar maximum —i.e. reaching the maximum number of sunspots in the cycle —there are increased solar flares and coronal mass ejections from the sun's atmosphere around the sunspots. These cause more cloud cover and colder temperatures on Earth.

Based on sunspot trends we should be in *a little ice age* by 2030 at the latest. It has nothing to do with burning fossil fuels. In fact we are going to need to burn a lot more fossil fuels if we are going to survive this. Prepare now. Prep for the coming dark winter,[20] and get right with God.

Those in the church must choose to follow Jesus the Son of God, to forsake all their idols, and follow Christ alone. There is no compromise with sin. Those who do not yet know Jesus have a choice. Follow Christ or follow Satan! There is no in between, no "gray" alternative.

To those who follow Christ, we read in Daniel 12:1-3

*1 And at that time shall Michael stand up [that's the archangel], the great prince which stands for the children of your people: and **there shall be a time of trouble**, such as never was since there was a nation even to that same time: and at that time **your people shall be delivered** [meaning saved from hell and destruction], every one that shall be found written in the book.*

That's the Book of Life. Those who know Jesus Christ will have their names written in that book. Make sure your name is written in there.

2 And many of them that sleep in the dust of the earth shall awake, some to everlasting life, and some to shame and everlasting contempt.

This passage describes the final day of the Lord, which is coming fast. Who are those who are resurrected with shame and contempt? Perhaps those in the church who have not stood with Christ against sin. Those who were not willing to give their lives for Christ and their fellowman.

3 And they that be wise shall shine as the brightness of the firmament; and they that turn many to righteousness as the stars for ever and ever.

These are those who followed the Lord through the pandemic of the virus bioweapon, through all the COVID vax mandates, the resulting tyranny and continue to stand for the truth of the Living God.

REVELATION 14:13, the apostle John is speaking:

> And I heard a voice from heaven saying to me, Write, Blessed are the dead which die in the Lord from **hereafter** [*meaning from this moment in time*]: Yea, says the Spirit, that they may rest from their labors; and their works do follow them.

This passage reveals that some of us will die in the coming apocalypse but you can have **your own personal Great Reset**. The Scripture says:

> He that believes on the Son has **everlasting life**: and he that believes not the Son shall not see life; but the wrath of God abides on him. — *John 3:36*

Trust in the Lord Jesus Christ and you will have everlasting life. And that life can never be taken away from you no matter what happens. This is the good news!

10

THE OLIGARCHS' WAR AGAINST GOD

WHETHER YOU LIKE IT OR NOT WE ARE IN THE middle of a war against God. Satan is the great imitator and to the global oligarchs he is their god. Through one world government, and global control of the financial and monetary system, they plan to control every aspect of our lives. This will include a cashless society and digital implantable ID technology, and a social credit system as in China. Vaccine passports or health passes with QR codes are only the beginning.

The last book of the Bible, the Book of Revelation, gives us some clues as to what is going on here. It speaks of such a control system:

> *And he [an anti-Christ world ruler] causes all, both small and great, rich and poor, free and bond, to receive a mark in their right hand, or in their foreheads: And that no man might* **buy or sell,** *save he that had the mark, or the name of the beast, or the number [666] of his name.*
> —*Revelation 13:16-17*

Though this biblical passage is highly allegorical and employs much metaphor and symbolism, there is a suggestion that those who worship the globalist system, controlled by Lucifer, will gladly take some kind of mark (seal). The mere fact it is used to control commerce seems to tie it to something like a digital identity device.

It is worth noting that the Book of Revelation informs us that God seals His own children with a seal in their foreheads. Since Satan is only an imitator of God, the meaning here of *the mark of the beast* cannot be totally a device like an ID chip and digital wallet. It must also be related to the decision that those people will make to willingly follow Satan. This is all about choice and it could be the reason why so much coercion was used to get people to choose the experimental COVID-19 "vaccines".

God speaks of those in power using "sorcery" to deceive the nations of the world. The word "sorcery" in English is translated from the Greek word "pharmakia", from which we derive words like pharmacy and pharmaceuticals (Revelation 18:23). This COVID-19 "vaccine" is modern sorcery. The global oligarchs speak openly of their Luciferian plans:[1,2]

No one will enter the New World Order unless he or she will make a pledge to worship Lucifer. No one will enter the New Age unless he will take a Luciferian Initiation." David Spangler, Director of Planetary Initiative, United Nations, 'Reflections on the Christ', 2012.

*The present vast overpopulation, now far beyond the world carrying capacity, cannot be answered by future reductions in the birth rate due to contraception, sterilization and abortion, but must be met in the present by the reduction of numbers presently existing. This must be done by whatever means necessary." **Initiative for the United Nations ECO-92 EARTH CHARTER***

"A total population of 250-300 million people, a 95% decline would be ideal." Ted Turner, founder of CNN and major United Nations contributor, in an interview with Audubon magazine.

"Depopulation should be the highest priority of foreign policy towards the third world, because the US economy will require large and increasing amounts of minerals from abroad, especially from less developed countries." **Henry Kissinger**

In Revelation chapters 6, 8 and 9, we read of deaths from wars, famine, and plagues and also it would seem from the bioweapon shots / "toxxines" (Revelation 6:2). From those texts, if you sum together the fractions of the world population that are killed, depending on how you calculate it, somewhere between 8% - 33% remain after the mass extinction event. That is, about 67% - 92% of the world's population is killed off.

And this might surprise you. We believe this is God's program! God judges the world through the acts of evil men. They may worship Satan and believe that Satan is really god, yet the Creator of the Universe is the One who is actually in control. What comes next is what we call Jesus' "Great Reset". Because we have read the last chapters of the book, we know it is God who wins in the end. The Luciferian globalists – the synagogue of Satan – cannot win. But this is the end of the world as we know it. Globalists talk of their New World Order, but it is Jesus Christ's New World Order that is coming.

However, we need to go through some hard times to get to that glorious ending. Nobody really knows when exactly that will be, nor how far Satan will get via his minions in trying to set up his New World Order, with their currently defined "Great Reset," but we don't have to wait hopelessly to find out either. All of us, right now, can seek our own personal "Great Reset," as we wait for the return of Christ, and the ultimate defeat of Satan and the destruction of Satan's New World Order.

When Jesus first walked the Earth, many of his followers, called "disciples," expected that He was about to immediately set up his New World Order, bringing the Kingdom of God from Heaven down to Earth. But it wasn't time for that back then. Jesus Himself taught His followers how to pray including this: "Our Father in heaven, hallowed be Your name. Your kingdom come, Your will be done, on Earth as it is in Heaven."

But He also said to pray: "For if you forgive others their trespasses, your heavenly Father will also forgive you, but if you do not forgive others their trespasses, neither will your Father forgive your trespasses. (Matthew 6:9-15)

This is really the "Great Reset" that is within reach of all of us: a resetting of our minds and hearts, so that we can enter into the Kingdom of God right now, even before Jesus' Second Coming. The most common English term used in the Bible for this is "repentance."

In the Book of Acts we read:

> Repent, then, and turn to God, so that your sins may be wiped out, that times of refreshing may come from the Lord; and He shall send Jesus Christ, which was before preached to you. He must remain in heaven until **the time comes for God to restore everything**, as he promised long ago through his holy prophets. —Acts 3:19-21

Ultimately, with the politicians failing us, the courts failing us, the police failing us, there is only one real choice as we head towards Jesus' "Great Reset."

During the days immediately following Jesus' death and resurrection, His disciples were presented a choice to go the way of the crowd or join the ranks of the few who recognized that Jesus was who He said He was–the Son of God and the promised Messiah. They chose the latter. It was the minority view, and it meant resisting the majority view, which included that of the ruling class, and often suffering for it. We are being presented with the same choice now. Standing for truth has a cost. Choosing to follow Christ, becoming His disciple, brings us immediately into the Kingdom of God, but not without a cost. Consider the cost, but if you follow Jesus the Christ you won't be disappointed.

Fear not! You are free indeed! That freedom was given to you by the Living God not by earthly rulers. And no man can take that from you.

SOLI DEO GLORIA.

NOTES

PUBLISHER'S NOTE

1. Klaus Schwab & Thierry Malleret, COVID-19: THE GREAT RESET, World Economic Forum, Switzerland, 2020, pages 15,19.

FOREWORD

1. Al Tompkins, 'What is an oligarch?', *Poynter*, March 4, 2022, at www.poynter.org/reporting-editing/2022/what-is-an-oligarch
2. Linda Elder and Rush Cosgrove, *Critical Thinking, the Educated Mind, and the Creation of Critical Societies. Thoughts from the Past*, at www.criticalthinking.org/pages/critical-societies-thoughts-from-the-past/762
3. John Stuart Mill, On Liberty, 1859, published by Batoche Books, Kitchener, 2001, at 17.
4. John Stuart Mill, On Liberty, 1859, published by Batoche Books, Kitchener, 2001, at 16.

PREFACE

1. Benedict Brook, 'Three words that sent Dr Kerry Chant global', News.com.au, 11 September 2021, at www.news.com.au/technology/online/social/three-words-that-sent-dr-kerry-chant-global/news-story/726cb8758017c0ee8411a42cb2cbbf1a
2. Ibid.

1. THE GLOBAL OLIGARCHY'S NEOFASCIST AGENDA

1. Justin Haskins, 'Joe Biden's Disturbing Connection to the Socialist 'Great Reset' Movement', Fox Business, 23 July 2020, atwww.foxbusiness.com/politics/joe-biden-socialist-great-reset-movement
2. Michael Rectenwald, 'What is the Great Reset', Volume 50, Number 12, *Imprimis* (A publication of Hillsdale College), December 2021, 3.

3. Adolf Hitler, 7 October 1933, quoted in G. DeMar, *Ominous Parallel: The End of Freedom in America* (Stein and Day Publishers, 1982) 3.
4. Jonah Goldberg, *Liberal Fascism* (Broadway Books, 2009) 15.
5. Kaitlin Smith, 'Examining Nazi Environmentalism During Earth Week', *Facing Today*, 25 April 2019, at www.facingtoday.facinghistory.org/examining-nazi-environmentalism-during-earth-week
6. John Cornwell, *Hitler's Scientists: Science, War and the Devil's Pact* (London: Penguin Books, 2004) 173.
7. Ibid., 154.
8. Ibid., 24.
9. See: Kaushik Patowary, *Pervitin: The Wonder Drug that Fueled Nazi Germany* (amusingplanet.com, May 25, 2020)

2. THE GLOBAL OLIGARCHS' DEATH WISH AND THE WUHAN LAB LEAK

1. Jung Chang and John Halliday, *Mao: The Unknown History* (Vintage Books, 2007) 18.
2. Ibid., 480.
3. Paul Johnson, *Modern Times: The World From The Twenties to the Nineties* (Harper Perennial, 1992) 152.
4. Stuart Schram, *Mao Tse-tung* (Hamondsworth, 1966) 291. See also: Geoffrey Blainey, *A Short History of the 20th Century* (Penguin Books, 2005) 285.
5. Paul Johnson, *Modern Times: The World From The Twenties to the Nineties* (Harper Perennial, 1992) 546.
6. Ibid.
7. Jung Chang and John Halliday, *Mao: The Unknown History* (Vintage Books, 2007) 3.
8. David Rockefeller, 'From a China Traveller', New York Times, August 10, 1973, 31
9. Salvatore Babones, 'Wuhan Confidential', *Quadrant Online*, June 15, 2021, at www.quadrant.org.au/opinion/qed/2021/06/wuhan-confidential/
10. Frank Fang, 'Columbia Professor Who Thanked Fauci for Dismissing Lab Leak Theory Has History of Collaboration With China', *The Epoch Times*, July 8, 2021, at www.theepochtimes.com/columbia-professor-who-thanked-fauci-for-dismissing-lab-leak-theory-has-history-of-collaboration-with-china_3888543.html
11. 'Fauci was 'up to his neck' funding coronavirus research in Wuhan', *Sky News Australia*, September 19, 2021, at www.skynews.com.au/opinion/sharri-markson/fauci-was-up-to-his-neck-funding-coronavirus-research-in-wuhan/video/e6cd6ab64aa984a2142ee04c58427744
12. Ibid.

13. Jean-Louis Margolin, 'China: A Long March into Night', *in* Stephan Courtois et al (eds), *The Black Book of Communism: Crimes, Terror Repression* (Harvard University Press, 1999) 542.

14. Jung Chang and John Halliday, *Mao: The Unknown History* (Vintage Books, 2007) 18.

15. 'Population Control: Is It a Tool of the Rich?', *BBC News*, October 28, 2011, at www.bbc.com/news/magazine-15449959

16. Ronald Bailey, 'To Save the Planet, Kill 90 Percent of People Off, Says UT Ecologist', *Reason Magazine*, April 3, 2006, at www.reason.com/2006/04/03/to-save-the-planet-kill-90-per/

17. Steven Quay and Richard Muller, 'The Science Suggests a Wuhan Lab Leak', *The Australian*, June 7, 2021, at www.theaustralian.com.au/business/the-wall-street-journal/the-science-suggests-a-wuhan-lab-leak/news-story/07015d3c2a31e3c0f49c056c1c2f894d See also: Tom Ozimek, 'Experts Point to Damning Gene Splicing Evidence of Likely Lab Origin of CCP Virus', *The Epoch Times*, June 7, 2021 atwww.theepochtimes.com/experts-point-to-damning-gene-splicing-evidence-of-likely-lab-origin-of-ccp-virus_3847591.html

18. 'Former CDC chief Redfield says he thinks COVID-19 originated in a Chinese lab', *Reuters*, March 27, 2021, at www.reuters.com/business/healthcare-pharmaceuticals/former-cdc-chief-redfield-says-he-thinks-covid-19-originated-chinese-lab-2021-03-26/

19. Anamica Singh, 'Did US scientists try to suppress Covid-19 lab-leak theory? Ex-CDC chief claims so', *WION*, March 9, 2023, at www.wionews.com/world/did-us-scientists-try-to-suppress-covid-19-lab-leak-theory-ex-cdc-chief-claims-so-570228

20. Ibid.

21. Marty Makary, '10 Reasons we KNOW that COVID-19 leaked from the Wuhan Lab', *New York Post*, June 19, 2023, at www.nypost.com/2023/06/19/10-reasons-we-know-that-covid-19-leaked-from-the-wuhan-lab/

3. MAN-MADE GLOBAL FAMINE

1. Joseph Mercola, 'Elitists' Goal: Wipe Out Good Food', *The Epoch Times*, July 27, 2023, at www.theepochtimes.com/health/elitists-goal-wipe-out-good-food_4625303.html

2. Food security, sustainable agriculture and water management', *Government of the Netherlands*, at www.government.nl/topics/development-cooperation/the-development-policy-of-the-netherlands/food-security-sustainable-agriculture-and-water

3. Jesse Rintoul, 'Farming for the Future: Why the Netherlands is the second largest food exporter in the world', *The Dutch Review*, July 26, 2022, at

www.dutchreview.com/culture/innovation/second-largest-agriculture-exporter/

4. James Crisp, 'Netherlands to close up to 3,000 farms to comply with EU rules', *The Spectator Australia*, November 28, 2022, at www.telegraph.co.uk/world-news/2022/11/28/netherlands-close-3000-farms-comply-eu-rules/

5. Xin Du, 'The Dutch farmers' stand against green tyranny', *The Spectator Australia*, May 13, 2023, at www.spectator.com.au/2023/05/the-dutch-farmers-stand-against-green-tyranny/

6. Masooma Haq, Joshua Philipp and Roman Balmakov, 'Food Shortages Looming in New Future Due to Governments' Globalist Policies', *The Epoch Times*, 23 July 2022, at www.theepochtimes.com/dutch-government-accused-of-following-globalist-policies-which-will-lead-to-food-shortages_4608652.html?utm_source=open&utm_medium=search

7. Kenny Torrella, 'Sri Lanka's organic farming disaster, explained', *Vox*, July 15, 2022, at www.vox.com/future-perfect/2022/7/15/23218969/sri-lanka-organic-fertilizer-pesticide-agriculture-farming

8. 'Major Livestock Producing Countries Commit to Mitigate Methane in Agriculture', *Global Methane Hub*, at www.globalmethanehub.org/2023/05/17/major-livestock-producing-countries-commit-to-mitigate-methane-in-agriculture/

9. Mike Adams, '13 Nations agree to engineer global FAMINE by destroying agriculture, saying that producing food is BAD for the planet', *Natural News*, July 18, 2023, www.naturalnews.com/2023-07-18-nations-engineer-global-famine-destroying-agriculture.html

10. See: https://vk.com/wall238470814_1155

11. 'Now is the Time for a Great Reset', *World Economic Forum*, at www.weforum.org/agenda/2020/06/now-is-the-time-for-a-great-reset/

12. James Gorrie, 'Who Put the World Economic Forum in Charge of Everything?', *The Epoch Times*, January 19, 2023, at www.theepochtimes.com/who-put-the-world-economic-forum-in-charge-of-everything_4982165.html?utm_source=open&utm_medium=search

13. Ella Kietlinska and Joshua Philipp, 'COVID-19 Emergency Powers, Green New Deal Paving Way for 'Great Reset' Tyranny: Climate Journalist', *The Epoch Times*, September 20, 2022, at www.theepochtimes.com/covid-19-emergency-powers-green-new-deal-paving-way-for-great-reset-tyranny-climate-journalist_4741735.html?utm_source=open&utm_medium=search

14. 'Brazil as an Agricultural Powerhouse', *WeForest*, June 10, 2022, at www.weforest.org/newsroom/brazil-agricultural-powerhouse#:

15. 'Russia-Ukraine War Worsens Fertilizer Crunch, Risking Food Supplies', *NPR*, April 12, 2022, at www.npr.org/2022/04/12/1092251401/russia-ukraine-war-worsens-fertilizer-crunch-risking-food-supplies

16. Lisandra Paraguassu, 'U.S. Denounces Bolsonaro's Solidarity with Russia as Ukraine Crisis Brews', *Reuters*, February 18, 2022, at www.reuters.com/

world/us-denounces-bolsonaros-solidarity-with-russia-ukraine-crisis-brews-2022-02-18/

17. Sam Cowie, 'Ukraine War: Global Fertiliser Crunch Pressures Brazil's Amazon', *Al Jazeera*, 16 May 2022, at www.aljazeera.com/news/2022/5/16/ukraine-war-global-fertilizer-crunch-pressures-brazils-amazon

18. Jack Nicas, 'Good News for Food, Bad News for War: Brazil Buys Russia Fertilizer', *The New York Times*, May 8, 2022, at www.nytimes.com/2022/05/08/world/americas/brazil-russian-fertilizer-sanctions.html

19. Robbie Gramer, 'How Team Biden Tried to Coup-Proof Brazil's Elections', *Foreign Policy*, October 28, 2022, at www.foreignpolicy.-com/2022/10/28/brazil-elections-bolsonaro-democracy-biden/

20. Ella Kietlinska and Joshua Philipp, 'COVID-19 Emergency Powers, Green New Deal Paving Way for 'Great Reset' Tyranny: Climate Journalist', *The Epoch Times*, September 20, 2022, at www.theepochtimes.com/covid-19-emergency-powers-green-new-deal-paving-way-for-great-reset-tyranny-climate-journalist_4741735.html?utm_source=open&utm_medium=search

21. 'How to build back better after COVID-19', *World Economic Forum*, April 3, 2020, at www.weforum.org/agenda/2020/04/how-to-build-back-better-after-covid-19/

22. Masooma Haq, Joshua Philipp and Roman Balmakov, 'Food Shortages Looming in New Future Due to Governments' Globalist Policies', *The Epoch Times*, July 23, 2022, at www.theepochtimes.com/dutch-government-accused-of-following-globalist-policies-which-will-lead-to-food-shortages_4608652.html?utm_source=open&utm_medium=search

23. Ella Kietlinska and Joshua Philipp, 'COVID-19 Emergency Powers, Green New Deal Paving Way for 'Great Reset' Tyranny: Climate Journalist', *The Epoch Times*, September, 20, 2022, at www.theepochtimes.com/covid-19-emergency-powers-green-new-deal-paving-way-for-great-reset-tyranny-climate-journalist_4741735.html?utm_source=open&utm_medium=search

24. Grant Miller, 'Here's What the USDA Revealed to the American People About Future Food Shortages', *The Epoch Times*, June 26, 2023, at www.theepochtimes.com/heres-what-the-usda-revealed-to-the-american-people-about-future-food-shortages_5342683.html

25. Amy Nelson, 'Farmer predicts more food shortages, higher prices in 2023: Wake up and support local', *Fox News*, December 28, 2022, at www.foxnews.com/media/farmer-predicts-more-food-shortages-higher-prices-2023-wake-up-support-local

26. Charles C. Mann, 'The Book That Incited a Worldwide Fear of Overpopulation', *Smithsonian Magazine*, January 2018, at www.smithsonianmag.com/innovation/book-incited-worldwide-fear-overpopulation-180967499/

27. Melanie Phillips, *The World Turned Upside Down: The Global Battle Over God, Truth and Power* (Encounter Books, 2011) 300.
28. Peter Jacobsen, 'Is Having Children in 2021 Really 'Environmental Vandalism'', *FEE*, April 28, 2021, at www.fee.org/articles/is-discouraging-people-from-having-children-environmental-vandalism/
29. 'Securing a Sustainable Future for the Amazon', DAVOS 2020, *YouTube*, at www.youtube.com/watch?v=9XKm0MUIJQs
30. 'Estimates of historical world population', *Wikipedia*, at www.en.wikipedia.org/wiki/Estimates_of_historical_world_population
31. 'Evangelical Leaders Exploited by Global Warming – Population Control Lobby', *Acton Institute*, September 29, 2006, at www.acton.org/press/release/2006/evangelical-leaders-exploited-global-warming-popul
32. Ronald Bailey, 'To Save the Planet, Kill 90 Percent of People Off, Says UT Ecologist', *Reason Magazine*, April 3, 2006, at www.reason.com/2006/04/03/to-save-the-planet-kill-90-per/
33. Encyclopedia Britannica, at www.britannica.com/event/World-War-I/Killed-wounded-and-missing, and at www.britannica.com/event/World-War-II/Forces-and-resources-of-the-European-combatants-1939
34. See: 'Public Enemies', at www.toppublicenemies.blogspot.com/2015/12/top-25-mass-murderers-in-history.html
35. Jack Nicas, 'Good News for Food, Bad News for War: Brazil Buys Russia Fertilizer', *The New York Times*, May 8, 2022, at www.nytimes.com/2022/05/08/world/americas/brazil-russian-fertilizer-sanctions.html
36. Christina Lu, 'Russia's Invasion Unleashes Perfect Storm in Global Agriculture', *Foreign Policy*, March 24, 2022, at https://foreignpolicy.com/2022/03/24/russia-war-ukraine-food-crisis-wheat-fertilizer/
37. John Gideon Hartnett, 'Has World War III Already Begun?', *The Mises Institute*, 31 July 2023, at www.mises.org/wire/has-world-war-iii-already-begun

4. PUSHING HARD FOR WORLD WAR III

1. 'Assignat', *Encyclopaedia Britannica*, at www.britannica.com/money/topic/assignat
2. The FED liabilities data 1914-2023 was collected from quarterly reports found here: www.fraser.stlouisfed.org/title/h41-factors-affecting-reserve-balances-depository-institutions-condition-statement-federal-reserve-banks-83?browse=1910s
3. The FED M2 currency supply data from 1959 to 2023 is found here: www.fred.stlouisfed.org/series/M2SL
4. Professor Hartnett would like to thank Rafi Farber, the End Game Investor, for getting him started looking into the FED liabilities and for his valuable advice.

5. Peter Rutland, 'An Unnecessary War: The Geopolitical Roots of the Ukraine Crisis', *Wesleyan University*, April 9, 2015, at www.prutland.faculty.wesleyan.edu/files/2015/07/Geopolitics-and-the-Ukraine-crisis.pdf

6. 'John McCain Tells Ukraine Protesters: 'We are here to support your just cause'', *The Guardian*, December 16, 2013, at www.theguardian.com/world/2013/dec/15/john-mccain-ukraine-protests-support-just-cause

7. Dominick Sansone, 'How We Got Here: Ukraine', *The American Conservative*, March 5, 2022, at www.theamericanconservative.com/articles/how-we-got-here-ukraine/

8. Seumas Milne, 'It's not Russia that's pushed Ukraine to the brink of war', *The Guardian*, May 1, 2022, at www.theguardian.com/commentisfree/2014/apr/30/russia-ukraine-war-kiev-conflict

9. Isaac Chotiner, 'Why John Mearsheimer Blames the U.S. for the Crisis in Ukraine', *The New Yorker*, 1 March 2022, at www.newyorker.com/news/q-and-a/why-john-mearsheimer-blames-the-us-for-the-crisis-in-ukraine

10. John J. Mearsheimer, 'Why the Ukraine Crisis Is the West's Fault', *Foreign Affairs*, September/October 2014, 2.

11. Ibid., 3.

12. Seumas Milne, 'It's not Russia that's pushed Ukraine to the brink of war', *The Guardian*, May 1, 2022, at www.theguardian.com/commentisfree/2014/apr/30/russia-ukraine-war-kiev-conflict

13. 'NATO's response to Russia's invasion of Ukraine', *North Atlantic Treaty Organisation* (NATO), 23 September 2022, at www.nato.int/cps/en/natohq/topics_192648.htm

14. Ibid.

15. Ibid.

16. Katabella Roberts, 'Ukraine Parliament Votes in Favor of Restricting Russian Music, Books', *The Epoch Times*, June 20, 2022, at www.theepochtimes.com/ukraine-parliament-votes-in-favor-of-restricting-russian-music-books_4544405.html

17. Ibid.

18. Ibid.

19. Ukrainian Trump or a Firm President? Here are 10 Things about Volodymyr Zelensky', *Livemint*, February 26, 2022, at www.livemint.com/news/world/ukrainian-trump-or-a-firm-president-here-are-10-things-about-volodymyr-zelensky-11645878721738.html

20. Jack Bingham, 'Ukrainian President Zelensky is tied to Klaus Schwab, Justin Trudeau, and other Global Elites', *LifeSiteNews*, March 3, 2022, at www.lifesitenews.com/blogs/why-would-the-ukrainian-president-cite-justin-trudeau-as-an-inspiration/

21. Ibid.

22. Leon Kushner, 'Why are so many Idolizing Zelensky and Ukraine?', March 8, 2022, at www.grandmageri422.me/2022/03/08/why-are-so-many-idolizing-zelensky-and-ukraine/

23. Jack Phillips, 'Zelensky Announces Ban on 11 Political Parties', *The Epoch Times*, March 20, 2022, at www.theepochtimes.com/zelensky-announces-ban-on-11-political-parties_4349682.html
24. Ibid.
25. Ibid.
26. Katabella Roberts, 'Ukraine Parliament Votes in Favor of Restricting Russian Music, Books', *The Epoch Times*, June 20, 2022, at www.theepochtimes.com/ukraine-parliament-votes-in-favor-of-restricting-russian-music-books_4544405.html
27. 'Europe's Economy And Living Standards Are Plummeting', *Oriental Review*, September 19, 2022, at www.orientalreview.org/2022/09/19/europes-economy-and-living-standards-are-plummeting/
28. Ibid.
29. Ibid.
30. Ibid. Weimin Chen, 'Germany's (And Europe's Self-Inflicted Upcoming Energy', *The Mises Institute*, September 19, 2022, at www.mises.org/wire/germanys-and-europes-self-inflicted-upcoming-energy-crunch
31. 'Institute IWH expects more bankruptcies in Autumn', *NewsinGermany*, at www.newsingermany.com/institute-iwh-expects-more-bankruptcies-in-autumn/
32. Weimin Chen, 'Germany's (And Europe's Self-Inflicted Upcoming Energy', *The Mises Institute*, September 19, 2022, at www.mises.org/wire/germanys-and-europes-self-inflicted-upcoming-energy-crunch
33. Tom Ozimek, 'Steve Forbes Criticises Fed for 'Making People Poorer', Insists America Is in Recession', *The Epoch Times*, September 20, 2022, at www.theepochtimes.com/steve-forbes-criticizes-fed-for-making-people-poorer-insists-america-is-in-recession_4742005.html?utm_source=ai&utm_medium=search
34. Ibid.
35. Wayne Root, 'Here's Your "Red Pill" Moment About the Russian-Ukraine War', *Gateway Pundit*, March 6, 2022, at www.thegatewaypundit.com/2022/03/wayne-root-red-pill-moment-russia-ukraine-war/?utm_source=add2any&utm_medium=PostSideSharingButtons&utm_campaign=websitesharingbuttons
36. Ally Foster, 'Scott Morrison Condemns Russia in Call to Ukrainian President Volodymyr Zelensky', *News.Com.Au*, March 5, 2022, at www.theepochtimes.com/steve-forbes-criticizes-fed-for-making-people-poorer-insists-america-is-in-recession_4742005.html?utm_source=ai&utm_medium=search See also: 'Scott Morrison, Volodymyr Zelensky, Speak as missiles supplied by Australia arrive in Ukraine', *SBS News*, March 6, 2022, at https://www.sbs.com.au/news/article/scott-morrison-

has-spoken-with-ukrainian-president-volodymyr-zelenskyy-heres-what-they-discussed/b88u0172d

37. Victoria Kelly-Clark, 'Ukrainian Aid Corridor to Get Australian Protection', *The Epoch Times*, 10 July 2023, at www.theepochtimes.com/ukrainian-aid-corridor-to-get-australian-protection_5386728.html? utm_source=open&utm_medium=search

38. Victoria Kelly-Clark, 'Ukraine Defence Effort Gets $110 Million Boost From Australia', *The Epoch Times*, 26 June 2023, at www.theepochtimes.com/ukraine-defence-effort-gets-110-million-boost-from-australia_5356361.html

39. Adam Creighton, 'Ukraine Latest Target in Propaganda Blitz', *The Australian*, 17 July 2023.

40. Oliver Bullough, 'Welcome to Ukraine, the most corrupt nation in Europe', *The Guardian*, 6 February 2015, at www.theguardian.com/news/2015/feb/04/welcome-to-the-most-corrupt-nation-in-europe-ukraine

41. Thane Angus, 'Ukraine: Part Two of the Great Reset', *The Postil Magazine*, March 1, 2023, www.theguardian.com/news/2015/feb/04/welcome-to-the-most-corrupt-nation-in-europe-ukraine

42. 'Foreign aid to Ukraine a money laundering scheme, head of Chechnya says', *TASS*, January 8, 2023, at www.tass.com/politics/1559463

43. Thane Angus, 'Ukraine: Part Two of the Great Reset', *The Postil Magazine*, March 1, 2023, www.thepostil.com/ukraine-part-two-of-the-great-reset/

44. Jack Bingham, 'Ukrainian President Zelensky is tied to Klaus Schwab, Justin Trudeau, and other global elites', *LifeSiteNews*, March 3, 2022, at www.lifesitenews.com/blogs/why-would-the-ukrainian-president-cite-justin-trudeau-as-an-inspiration/

45. Hugo Bachega, 'Ukraine War: Orthodox clerics say they will not leave Kyiv monastery', *BBC News*, 29 March 2023, at www.bbc.com/news/world-europe-65117269

46. Archbishop Silvester of Bilogorodka, 'An Open Letter to His All-Holiness Bartholomew, Archbishop of Constantinople – Ecumenical Patriarch', 12 April 2023, at www.kdais.kiev.ua/event/an-open-letter-12042023/

47. Archbishop Theodosy (Snigiryov) of Boyarka, 'If the Phanar Continues to Systematically Split Orthodoxy, Then Anything Can Happen', at www.orthochristian.com/125002.html

48. 'The Persecuted Church in Ukraine: Have We Lost Our Courage?', *Orthodox Reflections*, January 12, 2023, at www.orthodoxreflections.com/the-persecuted-church-in-ukraine-have-we-lost-our-courage/

49. Lucien Cerise, 'Wokism: The Engine of War in Ukraine and Poland', *The Postil Magazine*, March 1, 2023, at www.thepostil.com/wokism-the-engine-of-war-in-ukraine-and-poland/

50. Victoria Kelly-Clark, 'Ukrainian Aid Corridor to Get Australian Protection', *The Epoch Times*, July 10, 2023, at www.theepochtimes.com/ukrainian-aid-corridor-to-get-australian-protection_5386728.html

51. 'Keep standing with Ukraine and standing up to Putin', *Australian Financial Review*, July 4, 2022. www.afr.com/world/europe/keep-standing-with-ukraine-and-standing-up-to-putin-20220703-p5aypu

52. Rob Harris, 'Albanese promises Zelensky new $100m aid package during Kyiv meeting', *The Sydney Morning Herald*, July 4, 2022. www.smh.com.au/world/europe/albanese-promises-zelensky-new-100-million-aid-package-during-kyiv-meeting-20220704-p5ayrj.html

53. Katabella Roberts, 'Ukraine Parliament Votes in Favor of Restricting Russian Music, Books', *The Epoch Times*, June 20, 2022, at www.theepochtimes.com/ukraine-parliament-votes-in-favor-of-restricting-russian-music-books_4544405.html

54. 'The Fed is Shrinking Its Balance Sheet. What Does That Mean?', *Econ Focus*, Third Quarter of 2022, at www.richmondfed.org/publications/research/econ_focus/2022/q3_federal_reserve

5. SAVE THE PLANET, SACRIFICE YOUR CHILD!

1. Alexandra Marshall, 'Time and tithe: the Climate Cult's expensive virtue', *The Spectator Australia*, 19 June 2023, at www.spectator.com.au/2023/06/time-and-tithe-the-climate-cults-expensive-virtue/

2. Alexandra Marshall, 'Time and tithe: the Climate Cult's expensive virtue', *The Spectator Australia*, 19 June 2023, at www.spectator.com.au/2023/06/time-and-tithe-the-climate-cults-expensive-virtue/

3. See: Nicholas Goodrick-Clarke, *Black Sun: Aryan Cults, Esoteric Nazism and the Politics of Identity* (New York University Press, 2003) 4-5. See also: Melanie Phillips, *The World Turned Upside Down: The Global Battle Over God, Truth and Power* (Encounter Books, 2011) 233.

4. Rupert Sheldrake, *The Rebirth of Nature: The Greening of Science and God* (Batam Books, 1991).

5. D. James Kennedy PhD and Jerry Newcombe, *How Would Jesus Vote? A Christian Perspective on the Issues* (WaterBrook Press, 2008) 138.

6. 'Vast Majority of Evangelicals No Represented by Evangelical Climate Initiative', ECI Fact Check, Interfaith Stewardship Alliance, 2006.

7. D. James Kennedy PhD and Jerry Newcombe, *How Would Jesus Vote? A Christian Perspective on the Issues* (WaterBrook Press, 2008) 144.

8. Nell, Frizzell, 'Is Having A Baby In 2021 Pure Environmental Vandalism?', *Vogue*, 25 April 2021, at www.vogue.co.uk/mini-vogue/article/having-a-child-sustainable

9. Charles C. Mann, 'The Book That Incited a Worldwide Fear of Overpopulation', *Smithsonian Magazine*, January 2018, at www.smithsonianmag.com/innovation/book-incited-worldwide-fear-overpopulation-180967499/

10. Melanie Phillips, *The World Turned Upside Down: The Global Battle Over God, Truth and Power* (Encounter Books, 2011) 300.
11. Thomas Malthus, *Essay on the Principle of Population* (1798). Quoted from Melanie Phillips, *The World Turned Upside Down: The Global Battle Over God, Truth and Power* (Encounter Books, 2011) 224.
12. Charles C. Mann, 'The Book That Incited a Worldwide Fear of Overpopulation', *Smithsonian Magazine*, January 2018, at www.smithsonianmag.com/innovation/book-incited-worldwide-fear-overpopulation-180967499/
13. Peter Jacobsen, 'Is Having Children in 2021 Really 'Environmental Vandalism'', FEE, 28 April 2021, at www.fee.org/articles/is-discouraging-people-from-having-children-environmental-vandalism/
14. Deutsche Presse-Agentur, August 1988. Quoted from Melanie Phillips, *The World Turned Upside Down: The Global Battle Over God, Truth and Power* (Encounter Books, 2011) 229.
15. Prince Philip, foreword to *If I Were an Animal* (Robin Clark Ltd., 1886). Quoted in Melanie Phillips, *The World Turned Upside Down: The Global Battle Over God, Truth and Power* (Encounter Books, 2011) 300.
16. 'Prince Charles: 'Climate change to blame for terrorism', *News.com.au*, 24 November 2023, at www.news.com.au/technology/environment/climate-change/prince-charles-climate-change-to-blame-for-terrorism/news-story/bcf87d5197129873f933fc4e22c49ce0
17. Frank Barnaby, *The Gaia Peace Atlas* (Pan, 1988). Quoted in Melanie Phillips, *The World Turned Upside Down: The Global Battle Over God, Truth and Power* (Encounter Books, 2011) 302.
18. Normal Myers, *The Gaia Atlas of Planet Management* (Pan, 1985) Quoted from Melanie Phillips, *The World Turned Upside Down: The Global Battle Over God, Truth and Power* (Encounter Books, 2011) 302.
19. Paul Watson, quoted in Troy Mader, 'The Enemy Within', *Abundant Wildlife*, September 1992. Quoted in Melanie Phillips, *The World Turned Upside Down: The Global Battle Over God, Truth and Power* (Encounter Books, 2011) 302.
20. Chip Brown, 'She's a Portrait of Zealotry in Plastic Shoes', *Washington Post*, 13 November 1983, at www.washingtonpost.com/archive/local/1983/11/13/shes-a-portrait-of-zealotry-in-plastic-shoes/213e7fff-2221-4c35-bf9a-a850afd27200/
21. Katie McCabe, 'Who Will Live, Who Will Die' (1986) 21 (11) Washingtonian, at www.agris.fao.org/agris-search/search.do?recordID=US19900087948
22. Quoted from Melanie Phillips, *The World Turned Upside Down: The Global Battle Over God, Truth and Power* (Encounter Books, 2011) 303.
23. Charles Colson and Nancy Pearcey, *How Now Shall We Live?* (Tyndale House Publishers, 1999) 132.

24. 'Evangelical Leaders Exploited by Global Warming – Population Control Lobby', *Acton Institute*, 29 September 2006, at www.acton.org/press/release/2006/evangelical-leaders-exploited-global-warming-popul
25. Ibid.
26. Eric Lyons, 'Save the Planet ... Abort a Child!?', *Apologetics Press*, at www.apologeticspress.org/save-the-planetabort-a-child-2392/
27. Ibid.

6. TOTALITARIAN ROOTS OF THE ENVIRONMENTALIST DEATH CULT

1. Melanie Phillips, *The World Turned Upside Down: The Global Battle Over God, Truth and Power* (Encounter Books, 2011) 14..
2. John Stone, 'Global Warming Scare-Mongering', *National Observer*, 22 June 2006.
3. Vast Majority of Evangelicals No Represented by Evangelical Climate Initiative', ECI Fact Check, Interfaith Stewardship Alliance, 2006. Quoted from D. James Kennedy PhD and Jerry Newcombe, *How Would Jesus Vote? A Christian Perspective on the Issues* (WaterBrook Press, 2008) 1453
4. D. James Kennedy PhD and Jerry Newcombe, *How Would Jesus Vote? A Christian Perspective on the Issues* (WaterBrook Press, 2008) 144.
5. Melanie Phillips, *The World Turned Upside Down: The Global Battle Over God, Truth and Power* (Encounter Books, 2011) 17.
6. James Paterson, 'Tim Flannery: Climate Prophet', *IPA Review*, June 2011, 9.
7. 'How Green Were the Nazis', Ohio University Press, at www.ohioswallow.com/book/How+Green+Were+the+Nazis%3F
8. Kaitlin Smith, 'Examining Nazi Environmentalism During Earth Week', *Facing Today*, 25 April 2019, at www.facingtoday.facinghistory.org/examining-nazi-environmentalism-during-earth-week
9. David Blackbourn, *The Conquest of Nature: Water, Landscape, and the Making of Modern Germany* (Norton, 2006), 280.
10. Thomas Zeller, 'Molding the Landscape of Nazi Environmentalism: Alwin Seifert and the Third Reich', in: Franz-Josef Brüggemeier, Marc Cioc, and Thomas Zeller (Ohio University Press, 2005) 148.
11. Peter Staudenmaier, 'Advocates for the Landscape: Alvin Seifert and Nazi Environmentalism', Marquette University, May 2020, at www.epublications.marquette.edu/cgi/viewcontent.cgi?article=1284&context=hist_fac
12. Ibid.
13. Ibid.
14. Ibid.
15. Ibid.
16. Ibid.

17. Seymour Rossel, *The Holocaust: The World and the Jews, 1933-1945* (Behrman House, 1992) 79.

18. Melanie Phillips, *The World Turned Upside Down: The Global Battle Over God, Truth and Power* (Encounter Books, 2011) 228.

19. Anna Bramwell, *Ecology in the 20th Century*, 204.

20. Peter Staudenmaier, 'Advocates for the Landscape: Alvin Seifert and Nazi Environmentalism', Marquette University, May 2020, at www.epublications.marquette.edu/cgi/viewcontent.cgi?article=1284&context=hist_fac

21. Marc Cioc Franz-Josef Brueggemeier and Thoams Zeller, *How Green Were the Nazis? Nature, Environment, and Nation in the Third Reich* (Ohio University Press, 2005) 14

22. Melanie Phillips, *The World Turned Upside Down: The Global Battle Over God, Truth and Power* (Encounter Books, 2011) 228.

23. M Hawkins, *Social Darwinism in European and American Thought, 1860-1945* (Cambridge University Press, 1997) 139.

24. Richard Weikart, *Hitler's Ethics: The Nazi Pursuit of Evolutionary Progress* (Palgrave McMillan, 2009) 49.

25. Peter Saudenmaier, 'Fascist Ecology: The "Green Wing" of the Nazi Party and its Historical Antecedents', in: Janet Biehl and Peter Staudenmaier, *Ecofascism Revisited: Lessons from the German Experience* (New Compass Press, 2011) 29.

26. Adolf Hitler, *Hitler's Table Talk 1941-1944* (Oxford University Press, 1988) 341.

27. A Kolnai, *The War Against the West* (Viking Press, 1938) 241.

28. Ibid., 246.

29. Peter Staudenmaier, 'Advocates for the Landscape: Alvin Seifert and Nazi Environmentalism', Marquette University, May 2020, at www.epublications.marquette.edu/cgi/viewcontent.cgi?article=1284&context=hist_fac

30. Ibid.

31. Ibid.

32. Peter Saudenmaier, 'Fascist Ecology: The "Green Wing" of the Nazi Party and its Historical Antecedents', in: Janet Biehl and Peter Staudenmaier, *Ecofascism Revisited: Lessons from the German Experience* (New Compass Press, 2011) 29.

33. Paul Watson, 'The Beginning of the End for Life as We Know It on Planet Earth?', 4 May 2007. Quoted from D. James Kennedy PhD and Jerry Newcombe, *How Would Jesus Vote? A Christian Perspective on the Issues* (WaterBrook Press, 2008) 138.

34. Charles Colson and Nancy Pearcey, *How Now Shall We Live?* (Tyndale House Publishers, 1999) 132.

35. 'Evangelical Leaders Exploited by Global Warming – Population Control Lobby', *Acton Institute*, 29 September 2006, at www.acton.org/press/release/2006/evangelical-leaders-exploited-global-warming-popul

36. Don Feder, 'The Global Warming Suicide Cult', *Mannkal Economic Education Foundation*, at www.mannkal.org/downloads/environment/theglobalwarm ingsuicidecult.pdf
37. Ibid.
38. Melanie Phillips, *The World Turned Upside Down: The Global Battle Over God, Truth and Power* (Encounter Books, 2011) 229.

7. THE DIMMING OF THE SUN

1. 'Exposing the Global Climate Engineering Cover Up', *The Dimming*, You Tube, at www.youtube.com/watch?v=G_NYNt1I6-Q
2. 'GeoEngineering Watch', at www.geoengineeringwatch.org
3. Rob Waugh, 'Bill Gates backs plan to tackle climate change sun', *Yahoo! News*, 14 August 2019, at www.au.news.yahoo.com/bill-gates-backing-plan-to-stop-climate-change-by-blocking-out-the-sun-183601437.html
4. Ramon Tomey, 'Bill Gates' "block the sun" SCoPEx balloon launch experiment in Sweden hits a snag as environmental groups express criticism', *Climate Science News*, October 2, 2021, at www.climatescience-news.com/2021-02-10-scopex-ballon-launch-sweden-criticized-environmental-groups.html
5. 'Engineering: Stratospheric Particle Injection for Climate Engineering', *HandWiki*, at www.handwiki.org/wiki/Engineering:Stratospheric_Particle_Injection_for_Climate_Engineering
6. 'More gloomy news from Biden! White House says it's open to plan that would BLOCK sunlight from hitting surface of the Earth in bid to limit global warming', *Daily Mail Australia*, July 2, 2023, at www.dailymail.co.uk/news/article-12254167/More-gloomy-news-Biden-backs-plan-BLOCK-sunlight-Earth-bid-limit-global-warming.html
7. David Archibald, *The Past and Future of Climate: Why the world is cooling and why carbon dioxide won't make a detectable difference* (2010) 26.
8. Ibid., 7.
9. Dinesh D'Souza, *United States of Socialism* (All Points Books, 2020) 113.
10. Jonah Goldberg, *Liberal Fascism* (Broadway Books, 2009) 383.
11. Dinesh D'Souza, *United States of Socialism* (All Points Books, 2020) 112.
12. Ibid., 88.
13. 'Government Commitments to Climate Change', Australian Office of Financial Management, Australian Government, at www.aofm.gov.au/sites/default/files/2022-11-28/Aust%20Govt%20CC%20Actions%20Update%20November%202022_1.pdf
14. David Archibald, *The Past and Future of Climate: Why the world is cooling and why carbon dioxide won't make a detectable difference* (2010) 91.
15. Professor David Bellamy OBE, 'Foreword', in: David Archibald, *The Past and Future of Climate: Why the world is cooling and why carbon dioxide won't make*

a detectable difference (2010) 5.

16. V.M. Velasco Herrera, W. Soon, D.R. Legates, Does Machine Learning reconstruct missing sunspots and forecast a new solar minimum? (2021) 68(3) *Advances in Space Research* 1485-1501

17. J.G. Hartnett, BibleScienceForum.com, 27 May 2021, 'AI used to predict the next sunspot cycles: low solar activity until 2050', at www.biblescienceforum.com/2021/05/27/ai-used-to-predict-the-next-sunspot-cycles-low-solar-activity-until-2050/

18. J.G. Hartnett, BibleScienceForum.com, 27 June 2021, 'Grand Solar Minimums and the Fall of Empires: A Great Crash Looms', at www.biblescienceforum.com/2021/06/15/grand-solar-minimums-and-the-fall-of-empires-a-great-crash-looms/

19. 'Earth: Chemtrail conspiracy theory', *HandWiki*, at www.handwiki.org/wiki/Earth:Chemtrail_conspiracy_theory

20. Emma Siossian, Luisa Rubbo, and Claudia Jambor, 'Drought-affected farmers hit hard as freak hailstorm wipes out crops in NSW hinterland', *ABC News*, 18 September 2019, at www.abc.net.au/news/2019-09-18/hailstorm-wipes-out-crops-comboyne-nsw/11525316

21. Sue Allan and Nick Taylor-Vaisay, 'Literary off the charts: Canada's fire season sets records – and is far from over', *Politico*, 6 July 2023, at www.politico.com/news/2023/07/06/canada-fire-season-00104959

22. Flint Duxfield, 'Understanding the rare weather event that's flooded eastern Australia', ABC News, 11 March 2022, at www.abc.net.au/news/2022-03-11/understanding-the-rare-weather-flood-event/100900554

23. 'The Western Drought Is Bad. Here's What You Should Know About It', *The New York Times*, 21 October 2021, at www.nytimes.com/article/drought-california-western-united-states.html

24. U.S. Drought Monitor, Map released: 6 July 2023, at www.droughtmonitor.unl.edu/CurrentMap.aspx

25. GeoEngineering Watch, at www.geoengineeringwatch.org

8. EMERGENCY POWERS AND CLIMATE LOCKDOWNS

1. Author unknown.

2. Roiber Koppl and Abigail Devereaux, 'Biden Establishes a Ministry of Truth', *The Wall Street Journal*, May 1, 2022, at www.wsj.com/articles/biden-establishes-a-ministry-of-truth-disinformation-governance-board-partisan-11651432312

3. JD Heyes, 'Biden's former 'Minister of Truth' was a disinformation expert who took part in NATO-funded operations to deceive Europeans', *Natural News*, November 1, 2022, at www.naturalnews.com/2022-11-01-bidens-former-minister-of-truth-disinformation-expert.html

4. Charles Creitz, 'Canadian news outlet founder speaks out after Trudeau denies them journalism licence', *Fox News*, April 12, 2022, at www. foxnews.com/media/rebel-news-license-justin-trudeau-founder-speaks-tucker-carlson

5. Nabil Al-Nashar, 'Millions of dollars in fines to punish online misinformation under new draft bill', June 25, 2023, at www.abc.net.au/news/2023-06-25/fines-to-punish-online-misinformation-under-new-draft-bill/102521500

6. 'Communication Legislation Amendment (Combating Misinformation and Disinformation) Bill 2023, Australian Government, June 2023, at www.infrastructure.gov.au/sites/default/files/documents/communications-legislation-amendment-combatting-misinformation-and-disinformation-bill-2023-guidance-note-june2023_1.pdf

7. Dan Milmo, 'Legislation aims to shield UK interest users from state-backed disinformation', *The Guardian*, July 5, 2023, at www.theguardian.com/uk-news/2022/jul/04/legislation-aims-to-shield-uk-internet-users-from-state-backed-disinformation

8. Dr Silvia Behrendt and Dr Amrei Müller, 'The Proposed Amendments to the International Health Regulations: An Analysis', *Opinio Juris*, 27 February 2023, at www.opiniojuris.org/2023/02/27/the-proposed-amendments-to-the-international-health-regulations-an-analysis/

9. Dr Silvia Behrendt and Dr Amrei Müller, 'The Proposed Amendments to the International Health Regulations: An Analysis', *Opinio Juris*, 27 February 2023, at www.opiniojuris.org/2023/02/27/the-proposed-amendments-to-the-international-health-regulations-an-analysis/

10. 'Thanks To Pandemic, Climate Lockdowns Are Now On The Horizon', *Technocracy News & Trends*, June 14, 2023, at www.technocracy.news/thanks-to-pandemic-climate-lockdowns-are-now-on-the-horizon/

11. Mariana Mazzucato, 'Avoiding a climate lockdown', *World Business Council for Sustainable Development*, October 21, 2020, at www.wbcsd.org/Overview/Panorama/Articles/Avoiding-a-climate-lockdown#:

12. Dinah Voyles Pulver, 'Heat record after heat record will be broken in 2023. Here's how to make sense of it all', *USA Today*, July 9, 2023, at www.usatoday.com/story/news/nation/2023/07/09/2023-heat-breaking-records-climate-change/70384382007/

13. Forbes, 'July 4 Was Earth's Hottest Day In Over 100,000 Years—Breaking Record For 2nd Day In A Row', *Forbes*, July 5, 2023, at www.forbes.com/sites/maryroeloffs/2023/07/05/july-4-was-earths-hottest-day-in-over-100000-years-breaking-record-for-2nd-day-in-a-row/

14. 'The Sun Is Scorching The Earth With Intense Heat, And This Is Just The Beginning', *Before It's News*, July 16, 2023, at www.beforeitsnews.com/economy/2023/07/the-sun-is-scorching-the-earth-with-intense-heat-and-this-is-just-the-beginning-3090419.html

15. J.G. Hartnett, BibleScienceForum.com, 9 June 2017, 'A new Little Ice Age is predicted for 2030' at www.biblescienceforum.com/2017/06/09/a-new-little-ice-age-is-predicted-for-2030/

16. J.L. Casey, *Dark Winter, How the Sun Is Causing a 30-Year Cold Spell*, Humanix Books, Boca Raton, FL, USA, 2014.

17. 'Solar Cycle Progression', Space Weather Prediction Center, National Oceanic and Atmospheric Administration, at www.swpc.noaa.gov/products/solar-cycle-progression

18. A sunspot number prediction in the 11-year solar cycles requires assumptions and modelling. Another model predicts increasing sunspot numbers and the planet coming out of a cooling cycle, but observations trump models. Time will tell. See also John Gideon Hartnett, BibleScienceForum.com, August 15, 2023, 'Sunspots Affect Weather: Cycle 25 Surpasses Cycle 24' at www.biblescienceforum.com/2023/08/15/sunspots-affect-weather-cycle-25-surpasses-cycle-24/

19. Professor Richard Muller, 'Global warming bombshell – hockey-stick plot used modified data', *Bazzar Model*, November 24, 2004, at www.bazaarmodel.net/phorum/read.php?1,998

20. Ibid.

21. 'Solar Cycle Progression', Space Weather Prediction Center, National Oceanic and Atmospheric Administration, at www.swpc.noaa.gov/products/solar-cycle-progression

22. 'Significant Earthquakes – 2023', USGS, www.earthquake.usgs.gov/earthquakes/browse/significant.php

23. Nouran Salahieh and Melissa Alonso, '7.2 earthquake strikes off southern Alaskan coast, tsunami advisory no longer in effect', CNN World, July 16, 2023, at www.cnn.com/2023/07/16/americas/alaska-earthquake-tsunami-advisory/index.html

24. 'Magnitude 6.5 quake felt in Central America, no damage reported', *Reuters*, July 19, 2023, at www.reuters.com/business/environment/earthquake-strikes-el-salvador-reuters-witness-2023-07-19/

25. Roy Spencer PhD, 'Latest Global Average Tropospheric Temperatures', *Global Warming*, at www.drroyspencer.com/latest-global-temperatures/

26. C. Loehle, J. Huston McCulloch, January 1, 2008, Correction to: A 2000-Year Global Temperature Reconstruction Based on Non-Tree Ring Proxies, *Energy & Environment* 19: 93–100, available at www.journals.sagepub.com/doi/10.1260/095830508783563109

27. C. Loehle, December, 2007, A 2000 Year Global Temperature Reconstruction based on Non-Tree ring Proxy Data. *Energy & Environment* 18:1049–1058, available at www.journals.sagepub.com/doi/10.1260/095830507782616797

28. Steve McIntyre, 'On the Divergence Problem', *Climate Audit*, November 30, 2008, at www.climateaudit.org/?p=4475

29. Roy Spencer PhD, '2,000 Years of Global Temperatures', *Global Warming*, at www.drroyspencer.com/global-warming-background-articles/2000-years-of-global-temperatures/

30. Yan Zhang, Runze Li, Kaicun Wang, Journal of Hydrology Vol. 620, Part A, 129386, May 2023, 'Climatology and changes in internal intensity distributions of global precipitation systems over 2001–2020 based on IMERG', at www.sciencedirect.com/science/article/abs/pii/S0022169423003281

31. Ibid.

32. 'World Climate Declaration', *Global Climate Intelligence Group*, at www.clintel.org/world-climate-declaration/

33. 'World Climate Declaration: There Is No Climate Emergency – 1500 Signatories', *Global Climate Intelligence Group*, at www.clintel.org/wp-content/uploads/2023/02/WCD-version-02182311035.pdf

34. United Nations, 'Our Common Agenda Policy Brief 2 – Strengthening the International Response to Complex Global Shocks – An Emergency Platform', March 2023, 20.

35. U.N. General Assembly Resolution 76/307.

36. United Nations, 'Our Common Agenda Policy Brief 2 – Strengthening the International Response to Complex Global Shocks – An Emergency Platform', March 2023, 2.

37. Ibid.

38. Ibid., 22.

39. Ibid., 5.

40. Ibid., 19.

41. Friedrich A. Hayek, *Law, Legislation and Liberty*, Vol. 3 (University of Chicago Press, 1981), Ch. 17.

42. United Nations, 'Our Common Agenda Policy Brief 2 – Strengthening the International Response to Complex Global Shocks – An Emergency Platform', March 2023.

43. Graham Pinn, 'The un-United Nations', *The Spectator Australia*, June 14, 2023, at www.spectator.com.au/2023/06/the-un-united-nations/

44. Richard J Evans, *The Third Reich in Power: 1933–1939* (Penguin Books, 2006), 6.

45. Carl Schmitt, *Politische Theologie* (2nd ed, 1934), 20.

46. Jo Nova, 'Climate lockdowns coming? You will be tracked in your suburb and happy about it', at www.joannenova.com.au/2022/12/oxford-2024-climate-lockdowns-start-you-will-be-tracked-and-trapped-in-your-suburb-and-happy-about-it/

47. 'The surprising stickiness of the 15-minute city', *World Economic Forum*, March 15, 2022, at www.weforum.org/agenda/2022/03/15-minute-city-stickiness/

48. Isabella Fertel, 'Fact check: False claim UK city will test climate lockdowns in 2024', *USA Today*, December 23, 2022, at www.usatoday.com/story/

news/factcheck/2022/12/23/fact-check-no-uk-town-wont-introduce-climate-lockdowns-2024/10905558002/

49. Rhoda Wilson, '15-minutes: Councils are attempting to remove our freedoms, take control of our lives and herd us into spaces they completely control', *The Exposé*, February 12, 2023, at www.exposenews.com/2023/02/12/councils-are-attempting-to-take-control-of-our-lives/

50. WEF Official Admits 15-Minute Cities Will Imprison Humanity in Forever Lockdowns', *The People's Voice*, March 4, 2023, at www.thepeoplesvoice.tv/wef-official-admits-15-minute-cities-will-imprison-humanity-in-forever-lockdowns/

9. THE FOUR HORSEMEN HERALD THE MARK OF THE BEAST

1. Aimee Chanthadavong, 'Eftpos partners with major Aussie banks and retailers to launch QR code payments platform', ZDNET, October 12, 2021, at www.zdnet.com/article/eftpos-partners-with-major-aussie-banks-and-retailers-to-launch-qr-code-payments-platform/

2. 'MyGovID - An Easy and secure way to prove who you are online', *Australian Government*, at www.mygovid.gov.au/

3. 'Trusted Digital Identity Framework (TDIF)', *Australian Government*, at www.digitalidentity.gov.au/tdif

4. J.G. Hartnett, BibleScienceForum.com, 15 April 2021, 'Injectable microchip is not 'conspiracy theory'' at www.bibliescienceforum.com/2021/04/15/injectible-microchip-is-not-conspiracy-theory/

5. 'Bill Gates' 'Patent 666' Scares the World: Is It True Microsoft Has Acquired Intellectual Property To Microchip Humans With The Mark Of The Beast In Form Of COVID-19 Vaccine...', *The Grape Vine*, April 23, 2020, at www.thegrapevine.co.ug/bill-gates-patent-666-scares-the-world-is-it-true-microsoft-has-acquired-intellectual-property-to-microchip-humans-with-thwww.thegrapevine.co.ug/bill-gates-patent-666-scares-the-world-is-it-true-microsoft-has-acquired-intellectual-property-to-microchip-humans-with-the-mark-of-the-beast-in-form-of-covid-19-vaccine/

6. According to patentscope.wipo.int, Microsoft Technology Licensing LLC published patent number WO/2020/060606 on 26 March 2020 under International Application No.PCT/US2019/038084.

7. Fascism is actually a variant of socialism. The Fascist movement was originated in Italy by Benito Mussolini. Raised by a Marxist mother, at the age of 29 he managed to become one of the most effective and widely read socialist journalists in Europe. In 1912, Mussolini was elected the Head of the Italian Socialist Party at the Congress of Reggio Emilia, opposing parliamentary democracy and proposing that Italy should be thoroughly

Marxist. 'Marx', he wrote, 'is our father and our teacher' … He was a leading member of the revolutionary wing of the Socialist Party until Italy's entry into the Great War; then, he found himself in violent conflict with the Bolshevik-leaning leaders of his party. The coming of the war, coupled with his willingness to bring Italy into it, resulted in Mussolini losing his official position within the Italian Socialist Party. As a result, on March 23, 1919, Mussolini was compelled to create his own party, the Fascist Party, which nonetheless promised, among other things, the partial seizure of all finance capital; the control over all the national economy by corporative economic councils; the confiscation of church lands; and agrarian reform. See: Augusto Zimmermann, 'Adolf Hitler's Debt to Karl Marx', *Quadrant Online*, May 9, 2018, at www.quadrant.org.au/opinion/qed/2018/05/adolf-hitlers-debt-karl-marx/

8. Matthew O'Brien, 'Everything You Need to Know About the Cyprus Bank Disaster', *The Atlantic*, March 18, 2013, at www.theatlantic.com/business/archive/2013/03/everything-you-need-to-know-about-the-cyprus-bank-disaster/274096/

9. Skyler Caruso, 'Everything to Know About the Bud Light Controversy', *People*, 19 July 2023, at www.people.com/bud-light-controversy-everything-to-know-7547159

10. *Surveillance Legislation Amendment (Identify and Disrupt) Act 2021* (Cth), at www.legislation.gov.au/Details/C2021A00098

11. 'Pfizer To Require Twice-Per-Day COVID Pill Alongside Vaccines', *National File*, September 1, 2021, at www.nationalfile.com/pfizer-is-now-developing-a-twice-per-day-covid-pill-that-must-be-taken-alongside-vaccines/

12. J.G. Hartnett, BibleScienceForum.com,18 October 2022, 'We are Building Our Own Digital Prison' at www.biblescienceforum.com/2022/10/18/we-are-building-our-own-digital-prison/

13. Matthew Vann, Kaitlyn Folmer, Alex Hosenball, and Jinsol Jung, 'Blessing by way of medicine: These pastors preach COVID-19 vaccination as God's healing power', ABC News, March 15, 2021, at abcnews.go.com/Politics/blessing-medicine-pastors-preach-covid-19-vaccination-gods/story?id=76367456

14. Brian Shilhavy, 'Fully Vaccinated Franklin Graham Has Heat Surgery for Pericarditis as Samaritan's Purse Helps Inject People with COVID-19 Shots', *Vaccine Impact*, November 21, 2021, at www.vaccineimpact.com/2021/fully-vaccinated-franklin-graham-has-heart-surgery-for-pericarditis-as-samaritans-purse-helps-inject-people-with-covid-19-shots/

15. Daniel Y. Teng, 'Catholic Leader Issues Vaccine Mandate Across Australian Diocese', The Epoch Times, November 18, 2021, at www.theepochtimes.com/world/catholic-leader-issues-vaccine-mandate-accross-australian-diocese-4111027

16. Ibid.

17. Stop World Control, "Schools must equip children to have sexual partners" - say the UN and WHO, at www.stopworldcontrol.com/children/? inf_contact_key=183e33ed181dd9ba058265e457e-f26ab16358d5485884e2f31e6019a0d26c8b0

18. Ethan Huff, NaturalNews.com, 9 October 2021, 'Satanists admit that legalized abortion is how they perform ritual child sacrifices at the Satanic Temple', at www.naturalnews.com/2021-09-10-satanists-legal-abortion-ritual-child-sacrifices-satanic.html

19. J.G. Hartnett, BibleScienceForum.com, 19 June 2021, 'Global Cooling: Unprecedented Snow and Ice Gains in Greenland' at www.bibliescienceforum.com/2021/07/19/global-cooling-unprecedented-snow-and-ice-gains-in-greenland/; see also https://electroverse.info/

20. J.G. Hartnett, BiblieScienceForum.com, 29 March 2015, 'The coming long dark winter?' at www.bibliescienceforum.com/2015/03/29/the-coming-long-dark-winter/

10. THE OLIGARCHS' WAR AGAINST GOD

1. Sebastian Aguanno Jr., *truthandconspiracy.com*, December 17, 2020, 'Historical Quotes Regarding the United Nations, Lucifer, Agenda 2030, and New World Order' at www.truthandconspiracy.com/historical-quotes-regarding-the-united-nations-lucifer-agenda-2030-and-new-world-order/

2. Lisa Haven, *beforeitsnews.com*, August 29, 2016, 'We're Under Attack! Globalists Set 'Death Date' for World Depopulation' at www.beforeit-snews.com/alternative/2016/08/a-date-with-death-set-by-globalists-are-we-truly-under-attack-and-what-you-can-do-to-prepare-3405374.html

MORE BESTSELLERS
BY THE PUBLISHER

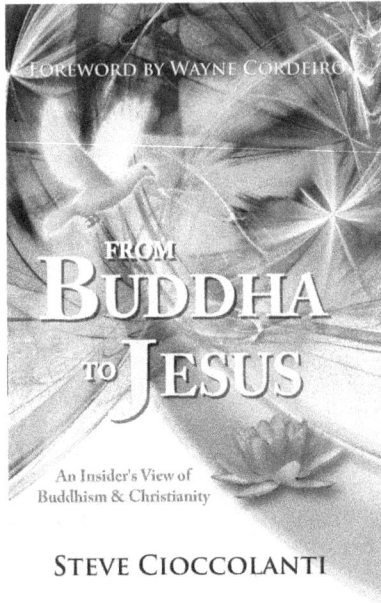

From BUDDHA to JESUS
(in English, Cambodian, Chinese, French, Hebrew, Indonesian,
Japanese & Thai)
#1 Bestseller throughout Asia
by Pastor Steve Cioccolanti

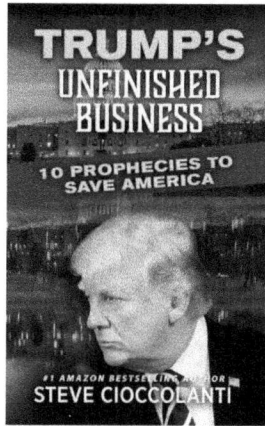

Trump's Unfinished Business:
10 Prophecies to Save America (378 pages)
(Paperback or Ebook)
By Pastor Steve Cioccolanti

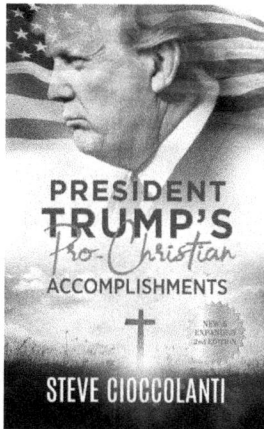

Trump's Pro-Christian Accomplishments (378 pages)
(Paperback or Ebook)
By Pastor Steve Cioccolanti

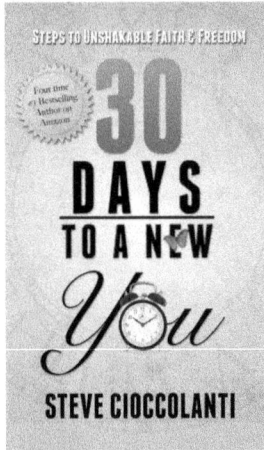

30 Days to a New You
(A Compact Plan for Personal Growth)

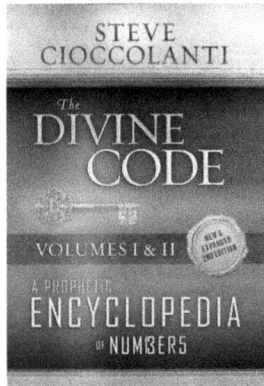

THE DIVINE CODE:
A Prophetic Encyclopedia of Numbers
VOLUME I (1 to 25)
VOLUME II (26 to 1000)

JUSTICE & RESTORATION
FOR CHRISTIANS

SCAM PROOF

YOUR LIFE IN THE END TIMES

STEVE CIOCCOLANTI

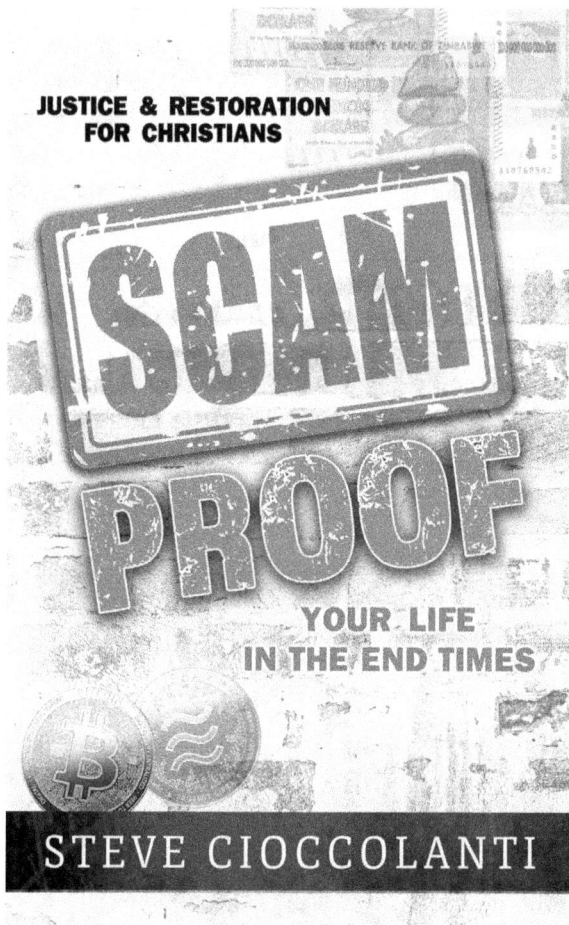

Scam Proof Your Life in the End Times (100 pages)
(Paperback or Kindle)

All e-books available through
Amazon.com/author/newyorktimesbestseller.

www.ingramcontent.com/pod-product-compliance
Lightning Source LLC
Chambersburg PA
CBHW060903280326
41934CB00007B/1165